Beetr
FOR BREAKFAST!

Tales and Memories of the Land Girls of
Lincolnshire and Nottinghamshire

as collected by
John A Ward

Frontispiece Illustration
Entitled 'Anything to Oblige'
was drawn by Miss Molly Capes
(Ex Land Girl now deceased)

Back Cover Illustration
Hodsock Priory in Springtime
(Hodsock was a WLA Hostel during the war)

First Published in Great Britain in 2010 by Tucann Books
Text © John A Ward All rights reserved 2010
Design © TUCANN*design&print 2010*

ISBN 978-1-907516-05-4

Produced by: TUCANN*design&print*, 19 High Street,
Heighington Lincoln LN4 1RG
Tel & Fax: 01522 790009
www.tucann.co.uk

2

" This Book is dedicated to all the girls of the Women's Land Army and the Women's Timber Corps who served throughout the length and breadth of Great Britain at the time of our nation's greatest need. "

About the Author

John Ward was born in Lambeth but was brought up in Nottingham from the age of 5 years.

After leaving school at 16 he worked for a brief time at Gedling Colliery before joining the Royal Navy for the next 12 years. On completion of his service he served with Nottingham City police and Nottinghamshire Constabulary. On retirement from the police service he was employed as the Business Awards Officer for the Duke of Edinburgh's Award, Nottinghamshire, finally retiring again in 1999.

John is a married man with two children and four grandchildren and still lives in Nottinghamshire. He is a keen local historian and craftsman making 54mm metal toy soldiers. He has a lasting interest in the work of the Women's Land Army and it was tales told him by past land girls which prompted him to produce this book.

Contents

Acknowledgements

This book is based mainly on information gained from many sources on the subject and on the contributions of the people named on the following pages. My thanks are also recorded to the following for their enthusiastic help and assistance.

Nottingham Central Library Local Studies Dept. Staff.
St. Ives, Cornwall Local Studies Library Staff.
The Nottingham Evening Post.
The Lincolnshire Echo.
The Mansfield 'Chad'.
The Sleaford Standard.
The Retford Times.
The Newark Advertiser.
Inside Lincolnshire.
The Lincolnshire Poacher Magazine.
The Sheepwash Times.
The Best of British Magazine.
The Lincolnshire Heritage.
The Farming & Machinery Magazine.
The Boots Company, Nottingham.
www.womenstimbercorps.comlbackground info

I would like to thank Sir Andrew Buchanan Bt. H.M. Lord Lieutenant of Nottinghamshire and Mr Tony Worth. H.M. Lord Lieutenant of Lincolnshire respectively for taking the time to write the Foreword and Commentary for this book.

If I have forgotten to thank anyone else who has given me help and information then I apologise and blame the omission on poor memory and old age.

Whilst all reasonable steps have been taken to ensure that no breach of copyright has occurred, the author would like to apologise in advance for any inadvertent omissions or errors and would be pleased to receive comment where due in order that a full acknowledgement may be made in any subsequent editions of this book.

I would also like to record my thanks to my wife Maureen, who accompanied me over many miles throughout Lincolnshire and Nottinghamshire to meet and talk to 'the girls' . Finally to my daughter Philippa for proof reading my efforts, I'm sure she is much wiser for the experience!

My grateful thanks to all the contributors listed below, in alphabetical order, who have either been interviewed or have sent letters to me and so made this book possible.

Babura. Beatrice - S.Connellsville, Philadelphia, USA.
Bailey. Hilda - nee Hammersley - East Markham, Nottinghamshire.
Bannister. Marie - nee De Wael. - Branston. Lincolnshire.
Baston. Joan - nee Matthews. - Collingham, Lincolnshire .
Beeston. Muriel- nee Brain. - Whitwell, Worksop, Nottinghamshire.
Bell. Margaret - nee Short. - Branston, Lincolnshire.
Bellamy. Ivy-nee Hallam.-
Bennett. Margaret - nee Witt. - Barkston, Lincolnshire.
Bingham. Marjorie - nee Ball. - Collingham, Lincolnshire.
Bossoms. Marion nee Fuller. - Rainworth, Nottinghamshire
Bostock. Elizabeth - Basford, Nottingham.
Bradford. Lena - Billingham, Cleveland.

Caddoo. Eileen - nee Myers. - Branston, Lincolnshire.
Cannon. Ethel - nee Greenwood. - Skegness, Lincolnshire.
Chisnell. Jessie - nee Stone. - Sutton in Ashfield, Nottinghamshire.
Cobley. Miriam-nee Hopper.-
Coxe. Kath - nee Storr. - Collingham, Lincolnshire.
Curtis. Marjorie - nee Nixon. - Birchwood, Lincolnshire.

Draper. Marian - nee Dobson. - Gosberton Clough, Lincolnshire.
Dunlop. Joan - nee Bennett. - Toowoomba, Queensland, Australia.

Beetroot for Breakfast!

Edwards. Betty - nee Jerrem. - Sherwood, Nottingham.
Eggleston. Joan - nee Bailey. - Blidworth, Nottinghamshire.
Elliott. Barbara - nee Pearson. (Deceased) - Warsop, Nottinghamshire.

Firmin. Beryl - nee Bestwick. - Billigborough, Lincolnshire

Gardner. Betty - nee Limon. - Mapperley, Nottingham.
Greaves. Barry - re Murden. Audrey - nee Greaves (Deceased)
Goodenough. Marion - nee Stokes. - Scunthorpe, Lincolnshire.

Haigh. Miriam - nee Barr. - Milton Keynes.
Hatcliffe. Mary Rose re Sylvia Ratcliffe (Deceased) Nottinghamshire.
Henshaw. Jean - nee Daft. - Bilborough, Nottingham.
Hobbs. Mr W R - Spalding, Lincolnshire.

Ingram. Pat - nee Trickett. - Tasmania, Australia.

Jones. Jean - London.

Kent. Joyce - nee Charlton. - Arnold, Nottinghamshire.

Leith. Claire - nee Oats. - Truro, Cornwall.

Martlew. Joyce - nee Bailey. - Blidworth, Nottinghamshire.
Monk. Margaret - Pinxton, Nottinghamshire.
Morley. Hilda - nee Spencer. - Woodthorpe, Nottingham.

Noor. Iris - nee Eaton - Mablethorpe, Lincolnshire
Nix. Marjorie - nee Cromer - Runcorn, Cheshire.

Parnham. Violet - nee Smith - Collingham, Lincolnshire.
Parrott. Margaret - nee Oldham - Penryn, Cornwall
Price. Elaine - Old Bilsthorpe, Newark, Nottinghamshire

Saunders. Rita - nee Fox - Waddington, Lincolnshire
Sewell. Joan - Bunny, Nottinghamshire
Sharpe. Laura - nee Shaw - Stapleford, Lincolnshire
Shepherd. Joan - nee Lloyd. - Newark, Nottinghamshire.
Shepperson. Evelyn - nee Cubitt. - Cropwell Butler, Nottinghamshire.

Shirley. Jean - nee Knighton. - Sutton-cum-Lound, Nottinghamshire.
Smith. Mary - nee Frith. - Louth, Lincolnshire.
Stonybridge. June - nee Bacon. - Lincoln
Summerfield. Eileen - nee Touson, - Spalding, Lincolnshire.

Taylor. Jean - re Mavis Maltby nee Morley. - Sherwood, Nottingham.
Truman. Joyce - nee Boston. - Lowdham, Nottinghamshire.
Twells. Derek - Stamford, Lincolnshire.

Ward. Muriel - nee Wild. - Wollaton, Nottingham.
Welton. Betty - nee Rawlinson. Caistor, Lincolnshire.
Wilkey. Sheila - Spalding, Lincolnshire.
Wright. Elsie - nee Jackson. - Donington, Spalding, Lincolnshire.

I would like to thank Sir Andrew Buchanan Bt. H.M. Lord Lieutenant of Nottinghamshire and Mr Tony Worth. H.M. Lord Lieutenant of Lincolnshire respectively for taking the time to write the Foreword and Commentary for this book.

If I have forgotten to thank anyone else who has given me help and information then I apologise and blame the omission on poor memory and old age.

Whilst all reasonable steps have been taken to ensure that no breach of copyright has occurred, the author would like to apologise in advance for any inadvertent omissions or errors and would be pleased to receive comment where due in order that a full acknowledgement may be made in any subsequent editions of this book.

I would also like to record my thanks to my wife Maureen, who accompanied me over many miles throughout Lincolnshire and Nottinghamshire to meet and talk to 'the girls'. Finally to my daughter Philippa for proof reading my efforts, I'm sure she is much wiser for the experience!

Foreword
by Sir Andrew Buchanan
HM Lord Lieutenant of Nottinghamshire

"I first visited Hodstock in 1943 when the Land Girls were there. My Aunt and Uncle lived in half the house and the Land Girls were in the other half with their bedrooms in the attics. Because they took such good care of the house and garden, Hodstock emerged from the War unscathed, unlike the house occupied by the Army, so I owe a debt of gratitude to the WLA.

When we came to live at Hodstock in 1967 and opened the garden to the public we met several ladies who had been here and whose memories were still very clear. That inspired us in 1995 - 50 years after the end of the War - to have a gathering of as many who had been here who we were able to contact. We had a very happy tea party for about 30ex Land Girls and they loved going up to the attics remembering which their own rooms were during the War.

Last November (2008) we held two Tea Parties for Land Girls to celebrate that The Queen had given Medals to recognise their invaluable service in our time of need. I was pleased to see the Medals being proudly worn on those occasions.

I was delighted to learn that their hard work, dedication and loyalty are being commended in this new book. Girls throughout the country had risen to the call to back their nation in that time of need. Called to take the place of the men who were required for front line duties, the girls were quick to respond to help feed the nation whose food stocks had been depleted to just three weeks supply.

Many books have been written in tribute to the Women's Land Army, the Women's Timber Corps and the services given to many counties of England. This book is a tribute to the girls who served in the counties of Lincolnshire and Nottinghamshire.

Sir Andrew Buchanan
Hodstock Priory, North Nottinghamshire

Commentary
Women's Land Army
by Mr Tony Worth. HM Lord Lieutenant of Lincolnshire

"On 25th January this year (2009) I was able to welcome some of the ladies of the Women's Land Army in Lincolnshire on behalf of Her Majesty the Queen to a special service in Lincoln Cathedral. It was held to recognise their contribution to the war effort and the fact that the government had recently issued a specially designed badge for them. This event and the badge had been a long time coming, and it was sad that so many Land Girls were not able to be present either because of illness and age or because they were no longer with us.

Those who were able to be present would have remembered the slogan that attracted them to join up: "For a Healthy Happy Job, join the Women's Land Army" and so many did. I know that there were several working on my grandfather's farm which I and my son farm today and there were still Land Girls there in 1950 when the scheme finally wound up.

To put the scale of the effort in proportion, by 1944 there were over 67,000 Land Girls working on the land and another 13,000 in the Women's Timber Corps (The Lumber Jills) without whom there would have been a severe shortage of pit props for the coal mines.

Although Agriculture was a reserved occupation, many of the farm workers joined up in the armed forces. If the Land Girls hadn't filled the gap, because of the U-boat blockades there would have not been enough food to go around in a country besieged by war.

Their efforts between 1939 and 1944 in England and Wales helped in the following ways:
- Arable land increased in area by 63%.
- Wheat, barley and potato crops almost doubled.
- Oat production rose by two thirds.

- Total agricultural workers increased by 22% (nearly all Land Girls)
- Cattle numbers increased by 6%.
- Tractor numbers increased by 50% between 1942 and 1944.

With their help the nation was able to feed itself, and win the war. There was a tremendous spirit amongst them and it is a sadness that it took so long for them to be recognised.

There are many wonderful stories which illustrate the spirit and commitment of the Women's Land Army.

Peg Francis, from Grimsby has said: "I was very young and had never been away from home. I was frightened of cows, but had no fear of hard work. The people I met during those four and a half years were full of kindness and generosity and I'm still in touch with some of the girls now. The farmer was a great conservationist and taught us a lot about the land. I got to plant his first ever 'Pick your own' field. We were all volunteers and keen to serve our country, but the contribution has been forgotten over the years".

Another Comment from **Eileen Caddoo**, from Branston:

"I've always been a lover of the great outdoors so joining up was easy for me. I became part of a mobile gang travelling by truck between the farms of Peterborough. Some days it was wet and cold, we slept in a stable at Elton Hall and were constantly hungry and our limbs ached, but I absolutely loved it. It was exciting, a chance to get away from home and make new friends. They said that Jimmy Stewart and Clark Gable were posted nearby!

I feel the girls should be recognised for our hard work and willingness to do our duty in time of need. I doubt many youngsters these days would be so keen to volunteer for such work!"

And **Ann Johnson**, who lives at Tydd St Giles near Sutton Bridge, has said: "I was based on Lord Derby's Estate in Lincolnshire. There were 24 of us Land Girls as well as another group of Lumber Jills from the Women's Timber Corps. It was the hardest work I've ever done in my life and in all weathers too!

It is marvellous to get this recognition after all these years. There's only three of us from our group left now but I know we will wear the badge with pride and in memory of all those girls who we worked alongside." Wonderful testimony to the spirit of the Land Girls and that spirit lives on. Recently, the Prince of Wales was in Lincolnshire planting a mulberry tree. Having topped up the hole with soil, he was walking away as if finished when a voice from the onlookers called out: You haven't finished the job yet." He turned and said, "Well you had better come and help me". A lady wearing a Women's Land Army Badge stepped forward and together they tamped down the soil with their feet. It is fitting that the badge has been designed and distributed, albeit at a rather late stage, which recognises their contribution to the war effort. It symbolises the gratitude of the nation and I am sure that all those who have received one will wear it with pride.

Introduction

I would like to point out that this work was never intended to be, in any form, a history of the Women' Land Army, many books have been written by excellent writers on the subject. I have however had to refer to W.L.A history in order that certain points are clear to the reader.

My original intention was to collect personal interests and stories from the Land Girls who actually laboured in the fields of Lincolnshire and Nottinghamshire, or from local girls from those two counties who have a tale to tell. It is inevitable that other counties will be referred to as the stories unfold when local girls left their homes in Lincolnshire and Nottinghamshire to work in other counties. I have also referred in part to several works by many authors and I have used certain quotes and prose which (where known) I have acknowledged within these pages.

I would like to record my grateful thanks to all the 'ex. land girls' that I have had contact with whilst gathering material for this project. I have received letters from some and many others I have had the pleasure and privilege of meeting personally. From those meetings and letters I can safely say that they were and still are 'a breed apart'. I found these ladies to be extremely friendly and willing to tell of their service days, I found that they really became animated and alive when recalling those days. Their sense of humour is wonderful and their memories fantastic.

I asked the standard question after each interview, "Would you do it all again?" and with only one exception they all replied "Yes" With girls like these working on the Home Front during World War II, no wonder Britain was Great!

When I first began meeting and talking to the ex. land girls featured in this book, several of them told me stories which I am unable to attribute to individuals. More than a couple of those stories featured the food which they received at the hostels where they were accommodated. On the first morning at their hostels they were surprised to see beetroot on the breakfast table and the idea of having it for breakfast, "No thank you"

They quickly learned that the beetroot was intended for their sandwiches, which they made themselves and took in their lunch boxes to the fields where they worked each day. Beetroot sandwiches stayed moist during the long hot days when many other fillings, mainly cheese and paste soon became dry. Hearing this it became apparent to me that the title of this book should be **'Beetroot for Breakfast!'**

Where did this project start?

It was on 3rd March 2009, my wife and I were driving through Lincolnshire; (we live in Nottinghamshire), when we decided it was lunchtime. Looking for a suitable public house we approached the village of Dunstan only to find the access to the village and the pub was temporarily closed due to road works.

We drove to the next village of Nocton, a one time R.A.F housing estate near Nocton Hall and a military hospital. The village has recently expanded into a substantial spread of quality housing but alas – no pub. Quest onward, the village of Potterhanworth had a pub. but a lack of advertising led us to believe that it didn't serve meals.

Unperturbed we drove on towards Lincoln City and passing through the village of Branston, we saw it, - a pub, The Wagon and Horses' advertising main meals. It happened to be a Tuesday and the notice outside announced 'Tuesday is roast day.' We had hit the jackpot!

We parked and entered to be greeted with the sight of a room absolutely filled with pensioners. Not a seat to be had but the alluring smell of roast beef kept us standing near the bar patiently waiting for a table to become vacant. That is when it really started!

Seated near the door round a table were three ladies who squeezed up and invited my wife and I to "come and join us", we accepted.

The three ladies duly introduced themselves to us and a most cordial lunchtime was spent in their wonderful company. During the exchange of conversation one lady stood out as a 'bit of a card', a description that was quickly endorsed by her friends. Marie was 90 years old with lots of stories to tell. As the customers began drifting out it became apparent that everyone knew Marie and as she was speaking with the departing clientele, one of the other ladies named Hazel told us that Marie had been in the Women's Land Army during World War II.

Now, being a man who spent 12 years in the Royal Navy I admit to knowing very little about the Women's Land Army. Looking back now I think very few of us really knew that much about it. We knew of it.

15

We think we know what they did but did we? Marie spoke for a while about some of her exploits and I soon began to take more than a passing interest in what she was saying. Marie then invited us to return to the Wagon and Horses, the following week when she would bring a couple of photographs to show to us.

The following Tuesday we again returned to enjoy another roast dinner and Marie invited us back to her home in Branston where she had a few interesting things to show us. We also met Sally, her Land Army doll.

After that meeting I was hooked. I did a little research on the Women's Land Army and apart from an official history by Vita Sackville –West there appeared to be little if any documentation about the Land Army in the counties of Lincolnshire and Nottinghamshire so I decided to make the effort to produce something to commemorate the remarkable work of the Women's Land Army and the Women' Timber Corps in those two counties, before it is too late. None of us are getting any younger!

I am pleased to say that we continue to see Marie on a regular basis and that lady is a tonic. Her stories and poetry have convinced me that I am doing a worthwhile thing in producing this work and I hope that my efforts will bring back some memories of the times when Britain had its back to the wall.

In January 2008, the government belatedly recognised the sterling work of the Women's Land Army in the form of a small certificate signed by Gordon Brown MP, Prime Minister and a Badge of Recognition, to all who served. Furthermore the right to representation at the Remembrance Day Service held at the Cenotaph at Whitehall each year - a small reminder of the huge contribution made by so many women who faced the challenge on the Home Front during the dark unpredictable days of the war.

News Release - 28th January 2008

As from Monday 28 January 2008, female war veterans can apply to have their efforts recognised with a badge of recognition.

The badge will acknowledge those surviving members of the W.L.A. and the W.T.C. who worked on the Home Front to provide food and timber for the nation during WWI and WWII.

Hilary Benn - the Environment Secretary said,
"It is absolutely right that we at last recognise the selfless efforts these women made to support the nation through the dark days of WWI and WWII. This badge is a fitting way to pay tribute to their determination, courage and spirit in the face of adversity. I hope that as many eligible women as possible will apply for one"

Background to the History.
Like many people I was always under the impression that the Women's Land Army was formed soon after the outbreak of WWII, having started the research for this book I soon learnt otherwise.

World War I started on the 4th August 1914 when Britain declared war on Germany. At that time many people believed the war would be short-lived and would be over by Christmas. By the end of January 1915 it became apparent that it would last a very long time. Over 100,000 men had joined the Army leaving the land to do their duty for their country. Such was the drain on the agricultural world that farmers began to suffer problems. The Army granted agricultural leave to a limited number of soldiers allowing them to return to the land and assist with the harvests.

As I have already intimated in the Introduction, this is not meant to be a history of the Women's Land Army. So suffice to say at this stage that the W.L.A. as we think of it today, was formed early in January 1917.

17

Duties on the land had existed prior to this date and had grown from a plethora of women's organisations which had come into being due to the outbreak of war. For example, the W.D.R.C. (Women's Defence Relief Corps), formed in September 1914, sent women to work on the land so as to release men to join the fighting forces. The minimum wage at that time was 18 shillings (90P) a week

The women who responded to this call for 'national work spending holidays in the sun' were mainly teachers, students, shop workers and clerks. Several other organisations helped in a similar manner.

1917 saw the establishment of the Women's Branch of the Board of Agriculture and its aim to increase the supply of women workers to the land... Duly appointed officers oversaw the recruitment to and the management of the service and in March 1917 the women's Branch became part of the Food Production Department. It was then an appeal was launched for women to join the Women's Land Army and over 30,000 women responded. The criteria for their recruitment were that they must be under 21 years of age, single and have their parents consent. The commitment to the Service was originally for the duration of the war but this was later changed to a six or twelve month commitment.

The pay was 20 shillings*

(£1) per week and, after passing a proficiency test, this was raised to 22 shillings (£1.10p) per week in March 1918. It was raised again in April 1919 to 25 shillings (£1.25p) after training.

Many important jobs called for women to replace the men who were called up for National Service and the Women's Land Army was made up of 3 sections, agriculture, forage and timber. Girls chose the section in which they wanted to serve whenever possible and provided that they signed on for at least 12 months.

The forage and timber sections were inter-changeable. A recruiting leaflet described the sections as –

'Our Soldiers must have food'
Agricultural Section: "Milking, hoeing, harvesting, ploughing, care of stock and horses, general farm-work and tree planting."

Our Soldier's horses must have hay.
Forage Section: "work at hay stores, stacking and loading bales, chaff cutting for the Army under the Forage Section of the War Office.
No training required.

Our Sailors need wood for their Ships.

Our Soldiers need wood for their railways, their shelters and their aeroplanes.

"In order to provide timber for the Navy and the Army, women must help in this work"

Timber Section: Felling trees, sawing into lengths, stacking and carting. Training will be given when necessary and those selected for the post of Supervisor will be paid £1 a week out of which maintenance must be provided.

(Recruiting leaflet IWM LAND 6/14)

Recruiting literature went on to describe, sometimes in great detail, the type of work expected from volunteers stressing why girls should join. Examples used were that "every girl loves horses", everything depends on their (the girls) health and strength", phrases used to entice the girls of Britain to sign up to the war effort.

Following the Armistice of 11th November 1918, women started to leave the Land Army and every Land Army Agricultural Section worker in

England and Wales was sent a letter from Muriel Talbot, Director of the Women's Branch of the Food Production Dept.

"Dear Landworker

Now the fighting has come to an end you will be wanting to know what is the position of the Land Army. Nothing certain can yet be said about the future, but one thing is certain, the whole world is very short of food and everything must be done to produce as much as possible.

Your Country still needs your help"

In May 1919, '**The Landswomen**'* published another letter further to the preceding one. Again Muriel Talbot wrote:

"I want all volunteers in the Land Army to know that their work is of as much value now as it ever has been. When the Armistice was signed, and we all rejoiced at the great change from war to peace. Many of you thought that your work on the land was over, but I want to show that it is not really at all. Many of the men who used to do farmwork have given their lives for the country or have become disabled in the service. Others are still wanted for the Armies of Occupation. So there is a serious shortage of labour and at a time of the year when the work must be done if the crops are to be secured and the necessary food supplied both for man and his beast. You came out to help your country... Go on giving your best – it is of real value and is greatly needed. I hope then that those of you who have reached the end of your term of service will enrol for a further period"

By October 1919 only 8,000 members of the Women's Land Army remained so Muriel Talbot wrote to them to say that the Government had decided that the Women's Land Army should be disbanded on 30 November.

Numerous letters and articles were written expressing the appreciation of the work undertaken by the girls of the W.L.A. stressing the hardships they had endured in those very hard and trying times.

Many members expressed their sadness at the demise of the W.L.A.; they would miss the companionship and happiness they gained from working as a team in the service of a common cause. Their loyalty and sense of purpose for extremely small rewards had been tested but they had won through knowing the value of their efforts and a rewarding outcome after the conflict.

• Note: 'The Landswoman' As membership of the W.L.A. grew, so did the need to communicate with its members. 'The Landswoman' was the monthly magazine of the W.L.A. and the W.I (Women's Institute) and was launched in January 1918 – Price 2d (1p) which increased to 3d in May 1918 due to rising print costs. It was available by personal subscription or from W.H. Smith. It carried agricultural news, health tips, verses, short stories, regular competitions and needlework etc. including items to encourage patriotism.

World War II
Early in 1938 it was becoming apparent that the dark clouds of war were again gathering. Having learnt lessons from WWI discussions were held at top level in the Government and the Ministry of Agriculture decided to appoint Lady Gertrude Denman in charge of the Women's Branch of the Ministry. Considering Lady Denman's experience in WWI she was well qualified. She had been Honorary Assistant Director of the Women's Branch in 1917 and had held the responsibility for recruiting for the Women's Land Army.

The civilian organisation known as the Women's Land Army was formed by June 1939 and was entirely staffed and run by women as it had been in WWI. Mrs Inez Jenkins was appointed as Assistant Director and was well known to Lady Denman in her appointment as General Secretary of the National Federation of Women's Institutes. The Headquarters of the W.L.A. was established at Lady Denman's country estate of 3,000 acres at Balcombe Place, Haywards Heath, Sussex.

The winter of 1939/40 was very severe and recruiting wasn't very good. Winter is the slackest time on the farm and although many women volunteered their services it really wasn't a good time to recruit them. By 1940 there were 6,000 land girls and according to the employment returns from 29 English counties, the following figures were obtained and included:

Hampshire	- 307 land girls employed.
Kent	- 222 land girls employed.
West Suffolk	- 187 land girls employed.
East & West Sussex	- 297 land girls employed.

By the following year the total had increased to 13,000 and the numbers continued to expand as did the range of work.

(figures from The Women's Land Army – a portrait by Gill Clarke)

Initially in December 1941, only single women between the ages of 20 and 30 were conscripted as announced by Winston Churchill but it soon became apparent that only total mobilisation of women couldn't be avoided.

A recruiting drive ensued and posters celebrated the wonderful life on the land. Clean, well turned out young ladies, nursing and feeding lambs, fit healthy women harvesting the crops in sunlit open fields were typical of the invitation to join the Women's Land Army. And what of the pay? Lady Denman had to fight long and hard to secure a minimum wage of 28 shillings (£1.40p) per week for the Land Army. Girls in reasonable office jobs in the towns were earning £4 per week! Out of their 28 shillings a week, a girl had to pay for her accommodation, around 14 shillings (70p)

Wages did go up during the war when the Ministry of Agriculture and Fisheries laid down that the W.L.A. should be paid a weekly wage of 32 shillings (£1.60p) if she was over 18 years old or worked over a 48 hour week. If she was accommodated in a farm house the wage was 16 shillings (80p) plus free board and lodging.

Before a volunteer went on a farm she would be told how the working week was made up and of the county rate of wages. She would also be told whether Sunday and Bank Holidays were counted as ordinary overtime or overtime at a higher rate. Holidays with pay were highly uncommon in pre-war years and Lady Denman and Inez Jenkins spent years of lobbying to receive a satisfactory result relating to this.

It may be of benefit to the reader to have an idea of costs in wartime Britain so here are some prices compiled by two girls working in Somerset

22

in the summer of 1940.

Rent	5/3d (27p)	Cocoa	6d (3p)
Coal/oil	3/7d (18p)	Coffee (Camp)	10d (5p)
Papers	11d (6p)	Milk	7d (3p)
Meat	3/8d (18p)	tin milk	7d (3p)
Bread	2/1d (21p)	soap, matches	1/1d (6p)
Marmalade	6d (3p)	cheese	6d (3p)
Jam	8d (4p)	sugar	7d (3p)
Flour	6d (3p)	dry fruit/veg.	4/7d (23p)
Margarine	6d (3p)	sundries	2/5d (13p)
Sandwich spread	7d (3p)		

- price comparison approx. **A Grand Total of £1.13s.1d (£1.66p)**
- (not much change from 28 shillings, later 32 shillings per week)
- Figures taken from **'They Fought in the Fields'** by Nicola Tyrer

As you will be aware these figures would vary at different billets in different counties.

The Newark Advertiser of 28 April 1995 ran an article on the employment of women in war work. After outlining the many occupations in which women were employed the following was written by Ti Warner – Local Studies Librarian, Newark.

"The Women's Land Army (W.L.A.) was a hard and underpaid way of helping to win the war: in modern terms it paid only £1.85 (increased to £2.85 in 1944) for a minimum working week of 50 hours – a week which became even more strenuous at harvest time. Even so, by the end of the war around 80,000 women had volunteered to join the service, working on farms the length and breadth of the country.

Many farms in the Newark area were recipients of such labour, with hostels for the women being established at Collingham (in Woodhill School) and Hockerton. Others were accommodated by their employers on the farm and the memoirs of one such land army girl Mrs Joan Jones who came to work in Nottinghamshire shortly after conscription in 1941 are preserved in the archives of the Imperial War Museum in London.

Labourers.
Mrs Jones narrative begins with a description of the contrast she and her companions found between her previous life in London and her new

Beetroot for Breakfast!

posting in the country. *"Our destination a remote farm was 2.5 miles from the nearest village....miles and miles, or as we were to learn acres and acres of lush green fields and shady, leafy trees but oh so far from the city (actually only 12.5 miles we discovered) We shared a comfortable old fashioned bedroom in a small cottage and we were catered for by the farm foreman's wife"* Their first day began (as every other subsequent day began) at 6am. Breakfast was served at 6am and they reported for work at the former's house at 7am.

Dressed in breeches, thick socks, heavy boots, light shirts, thick green jumpers and felt hats the girls were informed that their weekly wage was to be £1.18s. 0d (£1.90p) or less!

No concessions were made to the girls' hitherto easy life in the city and they were expected to undertake precisely the same work as the male farm labourers.

As the year progressed Mrs Jones lugged hay bales to feed the stock, picked, riddled and bagged potatoes and hand hoed acres of young wheat, barley and oats.

Following the harvest, the drab days of autumn brought even tougher tasks in the form of stone picking, kale cutting, digging out dock weeds and hedge plashing. As autumn turned to winter and snow and ice prevented work on the land, even more gruelling jobs were assigned to the Land Army girls – silage making and even road mending.

"Two of us", recalls Mrs Jones, *"ran an entire pig farm for weeks when the farmer was seriously ill. We helped the vets with artificial insemination and TB testing of cows and helped deliver lambs and milked cows."*

Dancing.

But life in the W.L.A. was not all work. When Mrs Jones and her friends were transferred to live in one of the W.L.A. run hostels she found a new social life which more than made up for the daily grind of farm labouring.

"Life was very different. We went out in groups – girls of an age – city souls together. Nights spent in the hostel meanwhile, could be amusing when a lot of the girls got together – singing around the piano or dancing to records I bought by collecting 2d (1p) a week from each member) played on an old wind-up gramophone".

The ending of the war in Europe in May 1945 brought great celebrations to the W.L.A. hostel as it did throughout the country and although some of

24

the girls began to pack their bags to leave for home, others realised that there was still important work to be done.

Total victory was still some months away, "Most of the girls" recalls Mrs Jones, "did not leave until after VJ Day (Sept. 1945) My own departure from the land came in 1947 – very sadly in some ways. Life in the city, for me at any rate, was never the same again".

* Note: 1 shilling = 5p. 20 shillings = £1.00

Here come the Girls

A recorded miscellany of live interviews together with newspaper clippings with ex. Land Girls when I visited them in their own homes all over Lincolnshire and Nottinghamshire.

The result is a fine collection of the ladies own experiences told in their own words.

Here come the Girls

One branch of the Women's Land Army was that of the Women's Timber Corps. (W.T.C.) known as the 'Timber Jills' or' Lumber Jills'

The W.T.C came under the Ministry of Supply as opposed to the Ministry of Agricultural and Fisheries, which was responsible for the W.L.A. They wore the same uniform but had a special green beret instead of the felt hat, and a Timber Corps. badge of 'crossed axes'.

Muriel Ward nee Wild of Wollaton, Nottingham
Muriel adequately describes life in the Timber Corps both from the work undertaken and the social side of the job.

"We are," says Muriel Ward "one of the best kept secrets of the war, (Nottingham Evening Post 20 March 1995) and its true that the Women's Timber Corps is not the first to leap to mind when talk turns to the Land Army, that was a force of females whose 'war efforts' involved a range of outdoor pursuits predominantly farming but including other industries equally vital both at home and on the battle front. Foremost among those alternative activities was timber.

Production of home grown timber was a priority during those war years when imported wood was at a premium since it was crucial that no shipping space should be wasted during the Battle of the Atlantic. At the same time the country was moving rapidly towards total mobilisation of manpower and the extra men required to work in the woods were needed even more urgently elsewhere. It was up to the women to step into the forestry breach and take over the felling, haulage, measuring and sawmilling which in the past had been traditionally almost exclusively men's work.

"We were classed as civilians, which meant we only got two travel passes a year and after the war we got no demob. holiday and weren't

given any demob. clothes" explains Muriel Ward, who joined the Corps at the age of 20. *"In fact it was only in the last two years were we issued with underwear, at one point we threatened to walk down Downing Street in our birthday suits in protest – but never quite had the nerve to carry it out"*

Timber Corps recruits came from a wide range of occupations, hair dressers, shop assistants, typists and clerks. Muriel worked for the Civil Service in Nottingham – a reserved occupation, so she had to apply for special permission to join the Land Army, which was granted in 1942. She was interviewed in Arnold and asked if she would join the Timber Corps – a new section of the Land Army which had only established six months earlier – and given a choice of training: measuring, felling, tractor driving or saw milling.

"I chose saw milling and absolutely loved it – even though my father said, I was little better than a factory girl!"

She was sent to a camp in Bury-St-Edmunds for training, where she learnt to handle 'huge' trees but where there was still time to relax – such as dances with the Highland Light Infantry, *"where they all wore kilts and we wore the trousers"*

At the end of four weeks the newly qualified candidates were sent to work up and down the country.

"My friends were posted to rally interesting places" says Muriel, "I was sent to – Bury-St-Edmunds!"

The Nottingham girl, Muriel and one other girl presented themselves to the manager of a saw mill to which they had been allocated, to be told *"I never wanted women working for me, but I suppose nothing can be done about it now"*

It was an off -putting start, but Muriel recalls her time at the mill with real pleasure. She worked on an electric rack bench operating a saw six feet in diameter, to cut great slabs of wood to size from tree trunks, after lifting them on to the bench with a new electric hoist nicknamed George by Muriel. *"Just cutting slabs all day long may sound monotonous but we had a great number of orders all for different types of wood, different lengths and widths and so it took some sorting out"* she remembers *"and it wasn't without its hazards – like when you hit a nail that had been hammered into the tree for fencing or something and the wood jumped all over the place. Worse, you had to get the saw doctor in to mend the teeth you had damaged. There were about six men in that mill with fingers missing – but I have to admit that it was just a coincidence, not one had lost them in the saw mill – which was probably just as well since I was in charge of first aid (as well as fire fighting) and I didn't have any qualifications, I just seemed quite intelligent!"*

After almost 18 months at Bury-St-Edmunds she was transferred back home and worked at Brown's Timber at Wollaton – long gone now. – where, to her sorrow, there was no rack bench. Instead she worked a planer, cutting smaller pieces of wood which were used for making horses' shafts, utility furniture (bending the timber to shape in

Women of the Timber Corps felling trees. (Photo. Women in History 1989)

steam) and bizarrely, hockey sticks. Later she also learnt to use a band saw – an exceptionally delicate operation for anyone without a sharp eye and a steady hand. Although she worked with five other women to start with, they all left and she was on her own among her male companions – but she says – *"I got more respect from those men than I ever did in an office"*

Other workmates included German prisoners of war, who were stationed at Wollaton Park and who arrived in a lorry to report for work each morning.

"They really enjoyed working with us and had all sorts of tales to tell. In the evenings we often walked them back to their camp – just me in charge of all these great big chaps – I never felt at risk at all"

Muriel left the Timber Corps in 1946 after 3.5 years service which she looks back on with great fondness. She still has two miniature chairs which she made on her band saw to remind her of those days.

"And I still", she says *"adore timber, I wish I was still working with it"*.

Beetroot for Breakfast!

Almost 50 years after the Women's Land Army was disbanded (November 1950) the following article appeared in the '**Nottinghamshire Now**' publication of May 1995.

"Land Army girls undertook general farm-work, market gardening and forestry and were billeted at hostels near farms. **Joan Sewell,** 76, of Weldale Farm, Bunny was just 22 when she became a Land Army girl. In fact she ended up marrying the son of the farmer whose land she worked at Lodge Farm, Whysall.   She told 'Nottinghamshire Now' about her memories

"I was a Mapperley girl and in 1941 was sent to a hostel in Bunny (Nottinghamshire) *called 'Memoirs de Ma Mere' – (Memories of my Mother).   The hostel was run by a woman called Mrs Reed and there were 32 girls in all and we were sent out to farms in the area I loved every minute of the work.   There was this tremendous feeling that what we were doing was very special to the war effort.*

I was sent to Lodge Farm in Whysall (Nottinghamshire). *The farmer bred Suffolk Punch horses so I used to help out with looking after them, mucking out the stables and working with the horses.   I also did a lot of general farm-work including hoeing and sugar beet and mango knocking – all this means is that when you've pulled them from the ground you knock the dirt off them and throw them onto a pile.   We used to be up at 6.30am to milk the cows or help with* general *chores.   I used to help make the silage.   There was a wonderful team spirit.*

We wore special outfits – a khaki shirt, a Sherwood green pullover and breeches which lased down the sides with woollen stockings pulled up over them to the knee.   On our feet we wore boots, or wellingtons when very muddy.   If we were going into town or somewhere special we'd wear shoes.   For really mucky work we wore dungarees with a belt and there were gaiters which fastened with a little strap.   Oh, I mustn't forget the round hat that had a brim to keep the sun off your face – which was invaluable in the fields.

In the evenings – usually at the weekends we would go to dances at Abbey Manor. I remember a group of us girls who had been doing the threshing one summer went to a dance. We used 'Outdoor Girl' make-up and I think there was some 'Boots No.7'.   My hair had a natural curl but some of the other girls would spend hours putting theirs in rollers to make it curl.   We used to dance with the soldiers who were stationed at Bunny. Of course there were admirers but I liked the farmer's son Les as soon as I saw him. He seemed very kind.   We were married in 1945 on May 5

– three days before VE Day. The mood was changing for the better, it was a wonderful time. There was a feeling of relief. No more blackouts. No more rations. I used to hear the bombers go over Mapperley when I still lived at home, it was terrifying.

When I got married I had to use my clothing coupons to get a wedding dress. It was turquoise with a gold studded collar and I wore it with a navy blue hat, shoes and gloves and held a bouquet of white lilacs. It was not unusual to wear a colourful wedding dress as every woman getting married at that time wanted to wear it again for best.

The end of the war was a very happy time as I was married to Les and it was the beginning of peacetime. We've never taken that for granted."
Les recalls *"I will never forget the first time I saw Joan. She had brilliant red hair – the same red as the Suffolk Punch we bred on the farm. She stood out among the other girls. I was very lucky indeed to have met her. She was a hard worker – as indeed all the other girls were – and I know my parents knew I had made the right decision when I asked her to be my wife. It seems strange that we are celebrating our 50th wedding anniversary this month* (May 1995) *Looking back it doesn't seem that long ago at all. We are lucky to have happy memories. For others they would prefer to forget the wartime".*

Marie Bannister nee DeWael - Branston, Lincolnshire

This is the lady that I have referred to in the Introduction to this book, the one who started my interest in the Women's Land Army.

At the age of 14 Marie was working in the Co-operative dairy in Eccles, Lancashire when she decided to join the Land Army at the age of 21. I have talked with Marie on many occasions and she always seems to remember something else! Marie is now 90 years of age (2009) with a fantastic memory and a great zest for life.

"I was exempt really but they let me go" she said, *"On my way there (to join the W.L.A.) I met* **Dora Gray** *and we were thrown into the back of the same lorry"*
There was little or no training at all in those days and the girls were literally thrown in at the deep end. They were expected to carry out whatever duties they were called to do. There was a supervisor at some farms and some of the girls were accommodated at the farmer's house and took their work from him.

Beetroot for Breakfast!

"I was sent to a hostel in Lincolnshire, Mere House, where there were about 40 girls who went out daily to the farms in the area".

Marie said she enjoyed her time in spite of some of the rules.

"If we arrived back at the hostel after 8.30pm there was no cocoa and if it was after 10pm we lost our late night pass. That pass was a weekly one".

The girls were allowed to go to the dances but had to walk back from Branston to Mere – a distance of about 3 miles. There was no transport until they bought us all a bike. *"Of course it was pitch black due to the blackout and we used to ride down these country roads and we couldn't really see a thing",* she said.

"When I first went to Mere, the first week, I was very worried. I was told that I had to take the horse to the village at the weekend, to be shod. Well it bothered me all week and one of the other girls asked me what the trouble was and I told her that I had to take the horse to the village to be shot and I had never seen anything killed before! I won't tell you what she said but she did explain to me that I had mis-heard the word 'shod' for 'shot' – well you can imagine my relief.

Another thing I remember that first week was the farmer sending us out into the field to find the fat hen. What he didn't tell us was that fat hen was a type of grass!"

When the farmer learnt that I had worked in a dairy, he sent me to work in the milking parlour, I hadn't milked before and I hadn't got a clue what I was supposed to pull!"

Marie served with the Land Army from 1940 and after the disbandment of the organisation she carried on working on the land for a further 20 years.

'Mind my Bike!'
Marie Bannister nee De Wael

'The Hills are Alive'
Peggy Doherty (believed) Mary Cooke nee Bissett and Thelma Burden nee Armstrong at Tan Hill

Margaret Monk   Pinxton, Derbyshire

On 22nd June 2009 I visited Margaret at her home in Pinxton; we spent a very pleasant couple of hours talking of her memories of time spent in service.

"I joined the Women's Land Army on 31st July 1943 and received directions to report to a farm at Aslockton in Nottinghamshire. I was stationed at a hostel at Hawksworth and travelled to the farm each day. Hawksworth was a W.L.A. hostel with about 32 girls living there. I remember we caught the train from Nottingham to get to Aslockton and all the girls used to work at the farms in that area. Hawksworth hostel was originally built to house soldiers before the Land Army moved in. The girls slept eight to a room, each room having four bunk beds and its own bathroom. It was quite comfortable.

One girl from London had hardly any information as to where she was going, she knew it was Hawksworth but that was about it. When she arrived in Nottingham she found that very few people had even heard of Hawksworth but eventually she was directed to the right bus which took her to Whatton and from there she had to walk 3.5 miles in the dark, in wartime, no street lighting and no road signs. She was only 17 and a half at that time.

The girls worked a 55 hour week (Monday until Saturday lunchtime), those who couldn't get home for the weekend had to pay an extra one and a half days board and lodging at the hostel.

I had a happy time working on the land and after the war finished and the W.L.A. was disbanded in 1950, I did work an extra 3 years at Johnny Rose's farm at Kilvington. In the past I had worked at farms in Cottingham, Tuxford and Farndon, living in hutments. I enjoyed most of the work on the farms especially to do with animals, milking and the like. The worst job was threshing; it was hard, long and dirty work. Clearing the chaff was a rotten job.

All in all the L.A. was a good life. We weren't given any training but there was nearly always a supervisor there to help us. We learnt quickly and worked well as a team". Asked if she would do it all again? Margaret replied, "Yes, I certainly would. I'm still in touch with a couple of the girls from Worksop".

Margaret Monk (Extreme left) and the girls at Hawksworth Hostel, Nottinghamshire

Lily Hamilton and Nancy Wright Margaret Monk at the front

Margaret Monk (aged 21 years)

Beetroot for Breakfast!

Lena Bradford   Billingham, Middlesborough

After hearing that I was collecting Land Army memories, Lena telephoned me in June 2009. She will not mind me telling you that at that time she was 97 years old.

Lena said, "I was never in the Land Army but I worked as a cook at a couple of hostels. I was at Hodsock Priory for three years working in the kitchens so I met many land girls. I was at 'Ye Olde House' in Blyth, North Nottinghamshire, just across the road from the church and I used to cycle to the hostel to do the meals for the girls. I got into trouble one morning when a policeman stopped me, he said "Can you read young lady?" and pointing to a road sign, "What does that say?

"Stop", I said. "Well why didn't you? he said, I said, "I put one foot on the ground." and he said, "Get off and don't be so cheeky." I have very happy memories of working at Hodsock Priory; the girls were great to work with".

Note: Hodsock Priory was never a priory! It was just Hodsock Hall until the 19th Century and there is a complete record of the owners of the Estate dating from the days of the Doomsday Book. The house was turned into a W.L.A. Hostel in 1942 until the duration of the war. The present owner is Sir Andrew Buchanan – the Lord Lieutenant of Nottinghamshire. Later Lena was transferred to Wolviston Hostel in Cleveland when she met Jean White who also wrote to me and sent a couple of photographs. Jean worked in Cleveland during her time in the Land Army and of Wolviston Hostel she said, "It was the best hostel in the country".

'Ye Old House' Hostel at Blyth, North Nottinghamshire

Margaret Bell nee Short.   Branston, Lincolnshire.
Although Margaret was born in Grimsby she has lived in Branston for many years. Margaret has written a couple of articles concerning the Land Army for the '**Lincolnshire Poacher**' 'magazine and these are reproduced - by kind permission of that magazine, in a later chapter 'Poetry and Pieces' of this book. Margaret said,

"When I first joined the Land Army I had no training at all. I was 18 and sent to a hostel in Woodenderby, Lincolnshire, but I was only there for one month, that was in 1943. They then sent me to Marehan-le-Fen where I was in lodgings in a village 2 miles from the farm".

Asked about those lodgings Margaret continued, "There were two of us in this room and my bed was under the window. The other girl, she was a big 'un, always wanted the window open wide. Well, that was no good to me because my bed was under the window and kept getting wet, so it became a battle, open, shut, open, and shut all the time. She soon got fed up with that so I won in the end!"

Margaret was employed in general farm work and had little or nothing to do with animals but she recalled, "One job I had to do was to mix chaff with chopped mangles and some red powder, some sort of protein I think – and sugar beet and then I had to take it to the dairy for the cows. I did get a job with horses, that were best of all, but I didn't work with any other animals.

"We had some German and Italian prisoners working on the farm and they were okay. We also had two woodmen they were great; they were at Mareham-le-Fen. We used to go to the village hall where the airmen held dances, there was an airfield at Moorsby, quite near. At the hostel we always got good food, nice breakfasts and fillings for us to make some sandwiches every morning. We were looked after pretty well. Thinking back it was solid hard work, morning till night but I loved it".

Margaret left the Land Army in 1948 after 5 years service.

Beryl Firman nee Bestwick   Billingborough, Lincolnshire
Beryl was born in Carlton, Nottingham and now lives with her husband Henry (aged 93 years) in Billingborough, South Kesteven, Lincolnshire. She describes herself as "a land girl who did no farming"! I visited the couple at their home in September 2009.

"I volunteered for the Land Army and I never worked on a farm! I was sent to a hostel on Birthorpe Road, Billingborough, a purpose built place for about 40 girls.

Beetroot for Breakfast!

Before going there I worked for William Holland, a hosiery factory in Nottingham. I was 17 when I joined and my uniform was sent to my home in Carlton. Anyhow, I had to come here (Billingborough) where I was met by Miss Lynn Forster – the Warden – a big gangling girl, I think she could cover two yards in one stride! She was a good warden. The main body of the girls were in a large dormitory. I got an upper bunk and my bunk mate, Honor Burton was on the bottom but my problem was how to get down". (Beryl is quite small in stature) "I tried using the utility dressing table to climb down but in the end I had to jump. There was a big coke fire in the middle of the dorm. Honor was on household duties but I was a bit of a law to myself and didn't get up until about 8am. The reason, well, at the back of the hostel was about two acres of land and the hostel was self sufficient and while the girls were taken to various farms around and about, I was responsible for two acres of land. I had about 50 fowls to look after plus the vegetables, we grew most everything ourselves. It was a satisfying job because you could see the end product. We never ate any of the fowls but I remember the Warden asked me if I could kill one that was sick. I'd never done that so someone else got the job. I did get the 'killer instinct' later on when I stamped on an earwig which had bitten my leg!

We had the Pioneer Corps stationed nearby at Horbling and some of the boys helped with the gardening.

On the final week we had a dance at the village hall and a lot of the girls went down, the rest of us stayed behind and sat talking when suddenly the heating packed up – what happens if it blows up? I went to put the fire out with cold water and finished up in hospital with burns to my face and arms and just one week before retiring. The stove had flashed back catching me full blast and I was in hospital for over a week. Well I did finish in 1944 but you know, if I could I would do it all over again.

When peace was declared everyone went a little mad. Locals, service personnel and Land Girls alike all congregated at the crossroads at the centre of Billingborough and danced the night away. What a long impressive line we made for the Conga!"

This newspaper clipping appeared in a local Lincolnshire paper, date and origin unknown.

Five Prizes For Nottm. Land Girl.

*'An outstanding success was scored by Miss Beryl Bestwick
(20) of the Women's Land Army, whose home is at 113
Standhill Road, Nottingham, at the Billingborough (Lincs)
and District Horticultural Show.*

*This was an open show and from the produce of the hostel
garden which she cultivates, she sent in seven entries.*

These won five prizes, as follows:-

First prize, broad beans; First prize, peas;

Second prize, potatoes; Second prize, turnips;

Second prize, mixed tray.

*Miss Bestwick has been in the W.L.A. about 18 months;
and this was her first attempt to win prizes with her produce.'*

The following article was taken from the Grantham Journal 27th February
1947:

'The" Green Jersey Girls" leave Billingborough'
CLOSURE OF THE LAND ARMY HOSTEL

*By the closing of Billingborough Land Army Hostel at the week-end, not
only has the agricultural community lost a valuable source of labour, but
the "green jersey girls" will be much missed in the life of the village.*

*Their cheery smiles endeared them to the villagers from the very
outset. Whether in the street, café, inn or dance- hall, the girls could
always be relied upon to enliven the sociability of the occasion and they
were ever ready and willing to give a hand in the promotion of social
events on behalf of charity and other deserving objects.*

*Built in 1940 to accommodate a personnel of upwards of 30, several
hundred girls have since passed through the hostel. The original batch,
representing all walks of life, came mainly from Bradford and other West
Riding towns and during their residence infused the Yorkshire dialect into
the local brogue.*

SETTLED IN THE AREA

*Quite an appreciable number of the girls, though not now wearing the
familiar green, remain in the Billingborough district having married
and settled locally. Others too, became the wives of European volunteer
workers from the neighbouring Y.M.C.A. camp at Horbling. They also
now live on various farms hereabouts and frequently visit the village to
renew old acquaintances.*

Beetroot for Breakfast!

During the 10 years the hostel was in being, no serious mishaps occurred to the personnel and during the war years when many Allied troops were stationed in the district the girls maintained a high standard of propriety.

Their last generous and much appreciated gesture was the promotion of a children's Christmas party and will long be remembered by the kiddies.'

That article goes to show how well the girls soon became an integral part of village life and how they were missed when the Land Army left their various postings.

Beryl Firman nee Bestwick (right) gardening at Billingsborough Hostel with her friend Margaret.

(Photograph courtesy of the Heritage Trust of Lincolnshire)

Betty Edwards nee Jerrem.   Sherwood, Nottingham.

Betty lives with her husband Norman in a bungalow in Sherwood and I went to their home to talk with Betty in September 2009. Betty was very proud of her time with the Land Army and the Badge of Recognition she had received.

Betty said "I started work in a shoe shop, Saxones, and then got a job at Boots – aqua-flavine section. Our holidays were always taken on farms so it seemed natural for me to join the Land Army, which I did, at the age of 16. I was really too young but I was accepted. I had seen an advert asking for volunteers at Beeston when I got off the bus going to Boots. Three days later my uniform was delivered and I was told to report to Kinoulton (Notts.) Hostel for training. I was there for two months learning fieldwork and dairy farming.

After the two months training I went to Mr Richardson's farm at Bleasby (Notts.) and I was the only land girl there. I helped with the general farm-work and in the dairy and later I had to ask for help with all the work I had to do. Two years later we got an Alfa Lavelle milking machine and a tractor – a Fordson N with a handle starter and what a kick back it had got.

Later on I went to a farm at Bassingfield (Notts.) while I was there I had to take a horse and float to Holme Pierrepont, quite a distance. I had to share a room there with the farmer's 13 year old daughter and one weekend when I was at home with my mother she said, "Come here" and she started looking through my hair, "You're crawling," she said, My head was infested with lice. Well, she took me back to the farm and showed the farmer. They washed my hair in sheep dip, my head was burning when they had finished!

I was told to do household duties, jobs in the house and getting the farmer his meals. This was against the rules; I wasn't there to do domestic chores. The food wasn't very good either, fat bacon, bread and butter for breakfast and Marmite sandwiches every day. There was a cold water pump in the kitchen, it wasn't at all comfortable but all in all I did enjoy my time."

Betty joined the Land Army in 1942 and left in 1946 after 4 years service. Betty had an invite from Sir Andrew Buchanan; Lord Lieutenant of Nottinghamshire to attend Hodsock Priory for afternoon tea and to receive her Badge of Recognition but unfortunately Betty had an operation on that day and therefore could not attend.

Betty has a lovely Land Army doll she has named - 'Betty' (what else could it have been?) made by Dorothy Taylor of Bridlington, Yorkshire. To date, Dorothy has made 262 of the Land Army dolls which are really excellent as can be seen from the photograph of 'Betty' I must add that Dorothy has now stopped making them due to failing skills and the difficulty in obtaining certain materials and life like dolls. She is still extremely busy visiting schools and other organisations giving talks on the Land Army which are backed by many visual aids including mice, rats and sheep!

'Betty' one of Dorothy Taylor's wonderful dolls who lives with Betty Edwards of Sherwood. Photo. John Ward

Betty Edwards nee Jerrem

Betty Edwards nee Jerrem (2nd from right) and friends at a reunion

Beetroot for Breakfast!

Hello Sailor! l to r: Iris Newbold (Hull), Millie Parker (Bridlington) and Dorothy Taylor (Bridlington), show thewy have still got what it takes!

Sir Andrew Buchanan Bt. Lord Lieutenant of Nottinghamshire with Joan Baston nee Mathews at the Hodsock Priory Reunion - Nov 2008

Betty Gardner nee Limon.   Mapperley, Nottingham

Betty joined the Women's Land Army on 1st June 1942 and worked on a private farm for the first six months of her service leaving to get married. Her husband was attending an R.A.F. course and Betty worked on a farm in North Marsden, Buckinghamshire. They shared part of a double fronted house, the other part being occupied by an artist George Mackenney who painted a lovely portrait of her...

Betty said, "When I joined the Land Army I was told to report to Clipstone (Notts.) Hostel, where the accommodation and the food was very good. The days were very long and the work was hard. We often had to have lights on to get home. We used to cycle to the local farms but we did get a bus at Ollerton Water Mill to take us to Edwinstowe, Warsop and other places further from the hostel".

During her time, Betty worked with Italian P.O.W, s "They were okay" she said, "just ordinary men wanting to get back home like our own men, it made me realise the futility of war"

We helped with the threshing, six girls and one man to the machine but only for two weeks at a time, the rest of the time was spent on other farm-work. On the stack, self preservation was important; working on the stack, in the chaff-hole or caving (getting the straw out of the machine) we disturbed lots of rats and used to stick them with a hay fork! I also remember German aircraft hedge-hopping, you would hear them and then they would just pop up over the hedges.

I actually went for an interview at the Technical College, West Gate, Mansfield on 25th April 1942 and collected my uniform later and joined on 1st June but received no training. I served until my release on 23rd March 1946.

I attended a reunion last year (2008) at Hodsock Priory and received my Commemorative Badge from the Lord Lieutenant. I think my service made me more assertive and that I 'grew up' during that time. My only regret is that I feel sorrow for the Land Army girls who have passed on not knowing that their service had at long last been recognised until it was too late!"

NOTE. Betty now is invited to attend local schools to relate her experiences and memories to the children.

Beetroot for Breakfast!

Eileen Caddoo nee Myers.   Branston, Lincolnshire

Eileen was born in the Leeds Workhouse and received her basic education in Leeds. On reaching the age of 18 years she opted to join the Women's Land Army. I visited Eileen at her home in Branston.

"I had to go for a medical," she said, "we had to go and see our own doctor, they gave us 5 shillings (25p) to see him and you had to have two straight legs – no bows allowed. We were measured for our uniform in Leeds and then sent to Elton Hall, Proby's Estate, near Peterborough. I was one of the mobile gang and we travelled anything up to 60 miles to various farms. We used to ride in a canvas backed lorry and it was always wet. I remember our truck driver was Ivy and she was married to an airman. The farmer was a nasty piece of work. We were always hungry, we got bread, marg. some sort of cheese and a flask of tea and we were out up to 14 hours a day.

There were about 40 girls at Elton Manor and the mobile gang as about 12. Nearby, at Upton Hall, James Stewart, the film star was billeted and there was a rumour that Clark Gable was there too.

We had to work with Italian prisoners of war and there was one there that wouldn't give me a moment of peace.

"Oh, Mama Mia, Mama Mia" he used to shout, this went on every time I saw him and this was because I had a rather big bosom!

We used to walk up a footpath near an airfield – Polebrook – and watch the R.A.F. and Yankee planes coming and going. One day on the footpath we found a leg with a flying boot still on it!

We used to go to dances and socials at Alconbury, Kingscliffe. My first job was at Molesworth where we chopped down trees and hedges to make way for the bombers. That's the place where later a Peace Camp was set up.

We didn't get any training; we just got on with things. I remember we were working for Dennis's – The Potato King of England and it was pouring with rain. There was some civilians working with us on peace work, they could come and go as they pleased but we just had to carry on. We complained and were told to use sacks to keep us drier so we packed it in and had to walk 5 miles back to Sleaford and we were stopped a whole days pay for that.

Dennis's used to keep race horses, I think they still do and once we had to paint all the fences white as a penalty for back-chatting.

We dreaded harvest time – long hours – always thirsty, no loos, working over the weekend and no overtime. There was much to grumble about but I did enjoy my time. I never went back to city life but settled here in Branston"

Eileen Caddoo nee Myers of Branston (aged 21 years)

The following is from Defra, UK-Farming. (c.2007) where Eileen Caddoo is quoted as saying, "I've always been a lover of the great outdoors so joining up was easy for me. I became part of a mobile gang travelling by truck between the farms of Peterborough. Some days it was wet and cold, we slept in a stable at Elton Hall and were constantly hungry, our limbs ached but I loved it. It was exciting and a chance to get away from home and make new friends.

I will definitely be applying for a commemorative badge as I feel the girls should be recognised or our hard work and willingness to do our duty in a time of need. I doubt many youngsters these days would be so keen to volunteer for work"

Elton Hall, near Peterborough used as WLA Hostel
Photograph – Eileen Caddoo

Joan Shepherd nee Lloyd.   Newark, Nottinghamshire

Joan lives with her husband Albert in special accommodation in Newark. I visited them in September 2009 and found them to be a lovely friendly couple

Joan told me her story. "I used to work as a tailoress after leaving school and the factory was taken over by the government. We had to make greatcoats and webbing then, that was in Manchester. I was just over 21 when I got called up for the Land Army. I wanted to do market gardening but there weren't any vacancies so I went into forestry, the

Women's Timber Corps. I was sent to Wetherby in Yorkshire, what a shock! We slept in single rooms with concrete floors but we shared a bath-house and a place for our meals. The meals were okay but our daily sandwiches were mostly cheese.

I got six weeks training at Wetherby but I had no boots and had to use my own shoes and some thick socks so I got lots of blisters. We didn't get any training for using machinery; we got as bill hook and one of those big two man saws.

After the six weeks training I was sent to Newdigate in Surrey and my first job was clearing bracken to get to the trees. It was torrential rain when I started on that work. There were some Canadians stationed nearby, the Canadian Dental Corps. they told us to go to them if we had anything wrong. We didn't have any machinery but men came in with cranes and lorries to move the trees after they had been cut down. Some of the Canadians had been lumberjacks and wanted to help us but that wasn't allowed.

The Canadians held dances and socials at Newdigate village hall so we got invites to go there. They had a four piece band and I used to sing at the socials.

I was later moved to Sussex and billeted out at 'The White House' which became a hospital. The people who owned it were in the timber trade and did a lot for it, raising cash for the East Grinstead Burns Unit.

We used to hear the doodlebugs going over and looking up we could see them, flames coming out of the back and when the sound stopped we dived for cover until we heard it explode.

Oh, I met Albert at one of the socials, he was a pianist. I remember going into Croydon to buy an engagement ring and seeing the houses with no roofs. We got married in Manchester, March 17th 1945. I got the last wedding dress in the shop and had to borrow a headdress.

Albert was in the R.E.s (Royal Engineers) and was doing mine clearance in Holland when he saw a tank enter a zone which had not been cleared of mines. He saw the tank blow up and my brother Bobby was in that tank. Bobby is buried in Holland"

Joan received her Badge of Recognition through the post and asked if, looking back, she would do it all over again, she replied, "Yes, we had some good times, some sad times and you tend to forget a lot of the bad ones".

Joan Shepherd and her brothers.
Bobby, Arthur and Billy.

Great Grandma and Granddad
visiting Bobby's grave in Holland.

Marian Draper nee Dobson   Gosberton Clough, Lincolnshire
Marian was most descriptive when I visited her at her bungalow home
in Gosberton Clough, a village in the Holland district of Lincolnshire. I
spent most of the afternoon in company with her and her husband; Marian
furnished me with 'An insight into life at a hostel'

"I joined the Women's Land Army in July 1942, from Doncaster
railway station I changed trains at Lincoln where I met with other girls
on their way to Surfleet station.   At the station we were met by an open
lorry. The driver helped us all up the steps and into the lorry where we
all sat on the floor and had our luggage on our knees. We were taken to
Spalding, our hair blowing and not feeling very happy about it.

We arrived at Holland House in the High Street and shown to our
rooms which were temporary. I had to share with other girls and we had
mattresses on the floor. We were called down for a meal and after getting
to know each other a little, a few of us went out to see what Spalding was
like. We only saw two or three people but not one man!

Next morning we got up at 5.30am and had a breakfast, cereal and toast. We had a packed lunch in a tin box given to us; it consisted of a cheese sandwich, corned beef, an apple and a flask of tea. We were then allocated out to various farms.

The farmer sent transport for us at 7.30am and on the farm I was allocated to where we would be picking raspberries. We were back at 4pm ready for a cooked meal at 5pm.

The evening was free but if we went out we had to be back by 10pm. and the next morning we had to pack our own lunch.

August Bank Holiday we had weekend leave and decided to hitch-hike, there were three of us. We set off up Pinchbeck Road and got just over the crossing at Park Road and decided not to do it so we went back and caught the train to Doncaster. That was the Friday night and we had to be back for Monday morning.

The huts at Surfleet – where we should have been in the first place – were ready so we were taken there that night. Oh Dear! No heat on in the dormitories, concrete floors, bunk-beds, then across the field to the wash-room, take a bowl to the outside tap, no hot water, then afterwards into the dining hut for breakfast.

We had a lovely Warden though – Mrs Valentine, and we had quite good meals too. We went to 'The Mermaid' for a bath – 9d (approx.4p) or to a house just down the road for one shilling (5p). We stayed at Surfleet until October when it was getting very cold and then moved to Gosberton, to Bank House. It was quite a change. Still no carpets on the floor or stairs but there was a fire in the sitting room. We had six armchairs, the others were hard bottomed so, if we missed the pudding at the evening meal we stood a chance of getting a soft seat! We had sing-songs around the piano in the evenings and when supper was put out, some of us packed our lunch. Food was limited because of rationing.

We had a variety of jobs to do – raspberry picking, there was strawberries, loganberries and some hoeing between the sugar beets. There was potato picking, by hand into baskets then empty them into a cart led by a horse: it was very tiring and back aching lifting baskets up all day. The sugar beet had to be gapped and singled and later in the year it had to be ploughed up with a horse and plough. We girls then went out with long handled knives and chopped the tops off and put them into heaps to be loaded into carts and taken from the field. Wet days we worked in the shed mending potato sacks.

I remember once we were sent to pick apples in the foreman's garden, climbing up the trees to get them. We thought it was a slow job so we decided to shake the trees and pick up the apples. The foreman was far from pleased when he saw us and we didn't half get a telling off for that.

When we were working in Gosberton we went on our bikes but if we were down the fen we went by a little car that the farmer provided. I was asked to have a go with the car so it wasn't long before we took ourselves.

We used to do threshing as well, I was put on the stack to lift the sheaves up onto the drum, that was quite heavy work and I was paid 5 shillings (25p) a week extra for that. In the summer time some of us would go to another farm and pull gooseberries at so much a bucketful or we would go pea pulling and get 1/3d (6d approx) per 40lbs bag. Our wages were £1.9s.9p 9(£1.49p) per week after stoppages.

Back at the hostel we were allowed two baths a week, on a rota which wasn't always suitable, but we could swap. I became Leader at the hostel and had to deal with complaints from the girls or from the Warden if she wasn't happy with the girls coming in late or smoking in the dormitories.

I got into trouble once and I received a letter from the W.L.A. Secretary"

WOMEN'S LAND ARMY
Holland County Committee
Tel: Spalding 3019
32 The Crescent
Spalding, Lincs.

MAK/EMP

Dear Miss Dobson

As Leader of Bank House Hostel, I think it is only right that you should hear that three girls have been reported to me, Olwyn Johnson and Gladys Cass for returning to the Hostel last night at 10.55pm and Mary Simpson was found smoking in bed at 10.25pm last night with a lighted candle beside her bed. You will appreciate that, apart from health reasons, it is impossible to allow smoking in dormitories, the greater danger is fire. I have written to the three girls in question, but as you now have your House and Social Committee, and I know the Committee wish to keep up a good tone in the Hostel. I felt that perhaps you would like to know about this and keep a watchful eye on offenders!

Yours sincerely
Mrs M A Kettlewell
County Secretary

Miss M Dobson
Bank House, Gosberton.

Following a short discussion about that letter and the restrictions placed upon the girls Marian continued, "We used to help with the Red Cross and British Legion dances at the village hall. We were allowed a late pass until 11pm on a Saturday night. If something was special we could ask for a late pass until midnight! The Warden would be stood in the hall just under the big clock. We would all go back together, one of the boys would look through the letter box and say "She's there in her dressing gown", so we'd take off our shoes and go up the stairs as quiet as we could because there was no carpet on the stairs. Once when it was snowing heavily, six of us had been on a night out and decided to get the late bus back from Boston, we had to get off at Sutterton and had to walk back, it was a bit weird and the snow was quite deep but it was a change from sitting in each evening".

Marian left the Land Army in October 1955, just after the war ended. She volunteered to join some three years earlier when she was employed as Despatch Clerk in Barnsley. Bank House Hostel is still in existence but it is currently a residential care home and Marian visits regularly. A commemorative Robina tree was planted in the grounds of Bank House in 1999.

Rita Saunders nee Fox.   Waddington, Lincolnshire
I visited Rita and her husband Alan at their home in Waddington on 28th October 2009. Alan used to be a farmer. I asked Rita about her early life and she replied,

"I was born in Yarborough but I left home at the age of 14 because I wanted to work with animals in the New Forest. I broke my wrist while I was there and had to return home to recuperate. After that I went to Bishops Stortford and worked with greyhounds.

I was 17 in October 1939 and volunteered for the Land Army, my first job was on a big dairy farm. I can't remember how many cows there were but I'm sure it was more than 50; it certainly seemed like it at milking time! I had to get up at 4am in the morning to get to the farm by 4.30 am to help the men with the milking. The farmer liked to milk the cows at 4.30 am and again at 4.30pm in the afternoon. By November, the days were very cold and it was so dark cycling to work that early in the morning. There were no street lights because of the blackout and my cycle lamp had to be very dim so that I could be seen by other road users but not powerful enough to be seen by enemy aircraft. I can remember one morning I was startled by a soldier pointing his rifle at my middle and shouting "who goes there, friend or foe?" I hastily told him I was a friend.

Before I had been there very long, I was asked if I would like to transfer to a poultry farm. The poultry farmer was a grumpy old man who didn't want a girl to work with him. However, I was sent there and we finished up getting along famously and he taught me a lot about looking after chickens.

The owner of the farm was Commander Lightoller and he owned a boat called the 'Sundowner' and during the Dunkirk evacuation he was responsible for rescuing 120 men off the beaches and getting them back to Dover. Commander Lightoller had been second in command of the Titanic when it sank after striking an iceberg. Luckily he survived. He was a very charming man and I was honoured to be his land girl.

The winter of 1940 was bitterly cold with lots of snow, I cycled 4 miles to the farm and 4 miles back again each day sometimes pushing my bike through the deep snow. The only place warm enough to eat my sandwiches at lunch time was in the chicken house with all the chickens clucking around me. My job was to help the poultry man to clean the hens out and to collect the eggs. There were about 2,000 hens so that meant lots of eggs to collect. Because of the war situation it became more difficult to get enough food for the hens and eventually Commander Lightoller decided to close the poultry farm down.

Opposite the farm was a large estate that was being used as a prisoner – of – war camp for Germans. The bailiff on the estate was asked if he knew a land army girl who would take charge of a small home farm. It was for someone rather special! It turned out that the land girl required was to work for the Duke and Duchess of Kent. I got that special job!

I had just 4 cows to milk but I had pigs to feed and clean chickens, ducks and turkeys to care for and 4 beehives to manage. I learnt how to extract the honey and how to put the bees to bed for the winter. A very happy time was in the spring when there were baby chickens, ducks and turkeys to rear... From time to time there would be baby pigs and the biggest number in one litter was 19! The normal size family was 10 – 12. It was delightful when cows produced calves, they were pretty, playful and had lovely brown eyes. I worked hard; the cows had to be milked twice a day, seven days a week, 365 days a year including Bank Holidays and Christmas Day.

The sad times were when pigs had to go to market and turkeys had to be killed for Christmas. Plucking turkeys was a ticklish job as the feathers got up ones nose and made one sneeze.

Sometimes in the hay making season I would go and help another farmer along with his other land girls and there would of course, be threshing when the corn-stacks were taken to pieces and fed into noisy filthy machines so the corn could be extracted and the straw that remained could be used as winter bedding for the animals. Today, most jobs are done with machines, including milking, but then it was all done by hand!"

Rita told me that she felt like part of the family whilst working for the Duke and Duchess of Kent. She attended the christening of Prince Michael and the funeral of the Duke who was killed in a flying accident. Important visitors came to the farm: Winston Churchill, General Smuts and others. One who made a particular impression was Lieutenant Philip Mountbatten who much later became the Queen's Consort Prince Philip. Rita said, "He was the only one who came at 7 o-clock in the morning and talked to us while we were milking."

Rita's sister was also a land girl and worked at Parsonage Farm, Lakenham. Paying a visit there one day Rita met Farmer Saunder's son Alan. The eventual out-turn was that Alan and Rita married in 1945 at Iver Church. Marriage meant that Rita had to resign from the Land Army.

The newly married couple then ran a milk round which they bought from Alan's father and Rita kept the books. They went on until there was a legal requirement for all milk to be pasteurised. The equipment was far too expensive for a small business so it was sold to United Dairies.

Alan and Rita then worked for Alan's father on his farm, growing wheat and corn. Rita said, "We bought the baby pigs in and put them by the fire, wrapped in a blanket and even put the oven on to keep them warm".

The couple eventually retired and settled in Lincolnshire. They have many fond memories of farming especially in the Slough area. "But, said Alan, - farming is no life today too much red tape, no fun in farming anymore. There used to be a whole gang of us in the hayfields, the women would bring out the tea and we'd have a good laugh. Now it's all done by one bloke with a machine".

Rita's only regret is that service in the Land Army didn't get the recognition it deserved until recently – 2008- 60 years after the war.

Rita Saunders and Alan on their wedding day with her Guard of Honour from a nearby Hostel

Another photograph of Rita and Alan Saunders wedding with Princess Marina on the right

Rita Saunders nee Fox carrying out her chores down on the farm

Beetroot for Breakfast!

Margaret Bennett nee Witt   Barkston, Lincolnshire

Margaret was 17.5 years when she volunteered for the Women's Land Army. Born in Eltham, South London she experienced life during the blitz and joined the Land Army in 1945. Margaret was a shop assistant prior to joining up. Private billeting was not always the soft option as she soon found out.

"I had to go to the doctors for a medical before going to be measured for my uniform, said Margaret, I can't remember where I went, somewhere in London. My uniform arrived at my home soon afterwards together with a railway warrant to go to Donington in Lincolnshire. The Hostel there had about 50 – 60 girls who went out to local farms to work daily. I went into private billets during the summertime and worked in the glass houses at Spalding during the winter.

At one private billet, Jack Wrae's Farm, I was greeted with "I didn't want no land army" and showed me to a bedroom at the back of the house. There were bare floor boards, no drawers or wardrobe. There was a camp bed which the Land Army had provided and there was a piece of string across the room. I asked him where I was to hang my clothes and he pointed to the string, "There". He had a 26 year old daughter and his wife used to watch her every move – and mine. On one occasion she was sent to the shop and I said I would walk with her. Her mother objected but I still went and she followed us. I saw her looking in the shop window. Her daughter said, "Don't look at her; she's just keeping an eye out!" She was 26; I don't know what was wrong with her mother.

One day I had a bit of an accident in my bedroom and broke the po, you know- the pot. I told the farmer's wife and I apologised and said I would replace it as I had seen them on the market. Just a plain white pot, not expensive at all. "You won't get one like that." she said. She kept on about it every meal time for two or three days, it was very wearing. Eventually a near neighbour heard about my living conditions and took me in to stay with her. She was lovely. I still worked at the farm though. Later on I moved to Donington to become a milk girl. The farmer had arranged a move for me in 1947. I was given a milk delivery round using a pony and float. 1947 was a very bad winter, the snow was deep and many roads were blocked but I managed to get all my deliveries done although it took me all day instead of just a couple of hours. I used to help with the milking too, using a machine. I used to wash the cows then put them onto the milking machine; the dairyman would take them off afterwards and see to the churns. The milk round was sold off later but I got more tips that Christmas because I had managed my deliveries in spite of all the bad weather.

I was told I would be going to Bratoft on a milk round there but this time it was using a bike. Some of the calls were too far really. One day I heard a 'pipping' outside. I lived in the farmhouse and my boyfriend Bob was outside in a car, he helped me with the milk round but, of course petrol was rationed and he was restricted to a 10 mile radius. Because of the distance involved I wrote to the Land Army Authority and asked to go to a hostel at Swineshead where I worked for a Mr. Tunnard at Wigtoft near Boston. During the summer I worked on the farm doing all sorts of jobs and because Mr. Tunnard wanted me to stay on I worked in the farmhouse in winter".

I asked Margaret about other people she had worked with and she recalled a couple of stories.

"When I was at Spalding we had some German prisoners-of-war working with us. We paired up and I worked with a German called Edgar, he was very nice. One day we were cleaning bulbs and putting the smaller ones in chitting trays. We had to put newspaper in to stop them falling through. One of the girls saw a picture of the King and Queen and stapled it to the wall. When the Germans came in one of then ripped it down, he was cursing in German, I could guess what he was saying!

We had an old roadman who used to leave his barrow, brush and shovel in the dyke where he finished each evening. He always did this so one evening, when he finished work and went home we played a trick on him. One of the girls went into the 'black hovel' – the dyke which we called the black hovel (toilet) for obvious reasons – she came back with a rope and we hoisted his barrow up into a tree. Next morning he came to get it – no barrow – he searched around asking everyone if they had seen it. Eventually the truth came out when he discovered the nearby 'barrow tree'. Well, just imagine".

Margaret married Bob in 1949 and they both continued to work, Margaret on the land and Bob as an inspector for a building organisation. Sadly Bob died of cancer some years ago.

Asked about her 4 years service in the Land Army, Margaret replied, "I loved it; I would do it all over again, gladly"

Beetroot for Breakfast!

Margaret Bennett outside her Hostel.

Edgar the German POW who was a very kind and gentle man.

Jean Shirley nee Knighton.   Arnold. Nottinghamshire

I went to meet Jean at her home in Arnold on 1ˢᵗ October 2009. Jean told me that she had worked in north Nottinghamshire and that her friend from Sutton-cum-Lound would be visiting her that morning.

Jean said, "I worked at the Meridian factory on Haydn Road, Sherwood when I was 17 then I went to another hosiery factory on Haydn Road, Richard Stumps that's when I volunteered for the Land Army. I had to go to somewhere on Chaucer Street in Nottingham.

Well, I first got posted to Sutton-cum-Lound, near Retford, in north Notts. I went to a hostel where there were about 30 girls. That's where I met your sister-in-law (Margaret Parrott nee Oldham) and Joyce Kent, who will be here soon.

We all did general farm-work on the many farms throughout the area and they used to drop us off from a lorry. We used to go to dances at the village hall where we were joined by soldiers from the camp at Ranby, a R.E.M.E. camp I think it was. There was a trio playing at the village hall when they had their dances.

I remember April 1947, we had some terrible flooding and I got sent to another hostel at Hockerton, near Newark then later to Bury St. Edmunds to attend a Home Craft Course – cooking and housekeeping, we couldn't work as the land was all flooded.

Another thing I remember was about 1949/50 a Land Girl was murdered at Newstead. Her name was Flo DeVito, she was married and had twins but they never caught who did it!"

At this point we were joined by Joyce Kent and her husband who had travelled from their home in Sutton-cum-Lound. The conversation became three-way and reminiscences flowed. I'm pleased to say that I was able to supply my sister-in-laws address in Cornwall as all three had worked together in the past at Sutton.

Both Jean and Joyce are proud owners of a Land Army doll made by Dorothy Taylor of Bridlington, as I have described in the interview with Betty Edwards.

Jean Shirley nee Knighton receiving her Medal of Recognition from Vernon Coaker MP

Joyce Kent nee Charlton. Sutton-cum-Lound, Nottinghamshire
Joyce and her farmer husband came down from Sutton-cum-Lound where
they live to talk to me at Jean's home in Arnold (Previous page). Joyce
joined the Land Army in 1946 and served for three years until 1949. Like
Jean, Joyce was a hosiery worker before joining the Land Army but not
at the same factory. At the age of 14 she was looking after three machines
for 11 shillings and six pence a week (57p).

"I remember the River Trent bursting its banks" she said, "The water
was up to the roofs of the buildings in Gainsborough, (Lincs.), there
wasn't any work we could do on the land then

Later when I was in Nottinghamshire I remember being told to take 100
sheep from Averham (near Newark) to Upton, quite a long way and we

walked it, all the way! It made a nice change from singling.

I did most jobs on the farm but I didn't do any potato picking. I did do hedging which was the worst job I ever did.

I went to one farm at Mattersley, which belonged to Fred Ruddock. I was there for 18 months looking after about 100 pigs; they were in sties, not like today where they are kept in fields. I had to do all the cleaning and mucking out, it was an endless job".

Joyce was 18 years old when she volunteered for service with the Land Army. Once again this is a story of a life-long friendship.

Sutton-Cum-Lound, Notts.
Top photograph (left to right) Joyce Kent
nee Charlton. Jean Shirley nee Knighton
Violet Willis (deceased)

Margaret Parrott nee Oldham
All four girls worked together at
Sutton-Cum-Lound

Hilda Bailey nee Hammersley.   East Markham, Nottinghamshire

Hilda was born in Newton, Derbyshire and was working for the C.W.S. (Co-operative Wholesale Society) in Huthwaite, Nottinghamshire prior to joining the Land Army in 1941.

Hilda explained to me that one of her life-long friends from her Land Army days was Audrey Ashworth; they were friends for 65 years. I was due to talk with Audrey two weeks before meeting Hilda but sadly Audrey passed away the previous weekend. Audrey had lived on a farm at Norwell, Nottinghamshire so she still had a connection with the land until she left us. I have included a couple of photographs of Audrey after speaking with her son-in-law who lives in Newark.

Hilda said, "I was stationed at Tuxford in north Notts. having joined up on 25th March 1941. It was a big hostel, about 40 girls and we were sent out to surrounding farms in the area to do general farm-work. I had had no training at all; I don't think any of us had. I didn't even have a uniform at first. I remember the Forewoman, a Miss Edna Oxley, she told us one day to bring in an old mac. from home. We did. It was so we could white wash the cowsheds!

The food was good. We had a good breakfast every day and there was always a good meal when we got back from the fields. I remember in the evenings we often fancied toast but we didn't have a toasting fork. We had some lovely dripping so we stuck the bread on the end of a poker, we had an open fire, it wasn't very successful, it kept falling off but in the end someone managed to get a toasting fork – problem solved.

Everybody hated threshing time because it was always us, the land girls who got stuck in the chaff hole, collecting the chaff in big bags and taking it away to the store. It got down your clothes and we were always itching and getting a rash.   Like I've said, there were about 40 girls at the hostel and we only had three baths between us! Imagine.

Audrey used to drive us out to the farms and four men used to come with the threshing machines. The men worked on the machines, we got the chaff hole. We had Germans, Italians and Americans working on the farms as well, they were okay. I think the Americans were volunteer workers from the airfield and they came to get to know the girls. We all did general farming. We worked at a farm in Boughton as well, hoeing potatoes and sugar beet. I remember one farmer; a Mr Smith at Tuxford gave me 2 shillings and sixpence (12.5p) after the threshing – for doing a good job. 2/6d in those days was good money.

When it came to entertainment we used to cycle 6 miles to Retford

Village Hall for the dances, there was an army camp nearly at Ranby. Just before D-Day we were working at Markham Moor when we saw the convoys passing by on their way south ready for the invasion."

Hilda's friend and workmate was Land Girl **Madge Betts** who was stationed with her for much of her service time. Madge was bridesmaid at Hilda's wedding.

Altogether Hilda served 5.5 years in the Land Army from 1941 until 1946.

Hilda Bailey's (nee Hammersley) Wedding day   *Hilda Bailey (right) with Madge Betts.*

Elsie Wright nee Jackson   Donington. Lincolnshire
Elsie was an easy person to talk to and had a ready story of her memories of the time she spent in the Land Army.

"Joining the Land Army was quite an escape for me. I wanted some freedom from a rather stern father – Mum was lovely. Dad did give his permission so I joined the Land Army in 1946, I was not quite 18. I instantly got the nickname of Frosty. At that time I was living in Lemington, Northumberland and was given a rail ticket to travel to Grantham. There I met eight other girls in uniform and we all caught another train to Sleaford. We were met there by a man who was driving a converted Rolls Royce ambulance and we were taken to Billingborough.

Beetroot for Breakfast!

The Warden, Miss Taylor-West, or was it West-Taylor, anyhow she met us and gave us our instructions for the next day.

The following day we were taken by lorry to Haverholme Priory and set on hoeing peas. During the lunch break in a walled garden I recognised a man who turned out to be from Lemington, he was training to be a professional gardener.

We worked with German and Italian POWs, they were alright, they used to paint our lunch boxes for us in exchange for a small piece of soap; they were stationed at Horbling, just up the road. During our time off we used to go to The New Inn at Billingborough and that's where I had my first drink and smoke. During that winter of 1947, the snow was very bad. There was no work on the land and helicopters were dropping bales of hay to the sheep in the fields.

After that I went to Folkingham, to an old 3-storey house. There were only ten girls there and I saw a notice which read, 'anyone wanting to learn milking apply ……..' I did back at Billinghborough and met a Miss Lynne Trenchard from somewhere near Leeds. The milking sheds were at Stave Green, between Billingborough and Folkingham, it was a commercial farm and I used to cycle there. The cows there, Jersey cows, were owned by a Mr Chapman and we learnt hand milking and milking by machine using an Alpha Lavelle and Gascoigne milking machines. The cow feed was allocated in relation to the milk yield of each cow.

The area was run by Agriculture and Fisheries from Sleaford and they wanted Lynne and me to learn to drive. It was about this time when the MMB (Milk Marketing Board) came into being and farmers were paid more if they were registered.

There was a 10cwt van stationed at Horbling Camp and when farmers wanted calves from a registered bull we took it to the farm in the van. We also collected milk in churns and took it to the depot and were responsible for cleaning the milking machines and all the utensils.

We used to help out at various other farms and I went to help with mangold-wurzel chopping for Commander Ballard RN. as his man had chopped off two of his own fingers. This was at Allington near Grantham. I did the milking and lived there for a year. I was paid once a month – a £5 cheque. Once a week they took me to the pictures in Grantham, they had no family and I got very few weekends off. Her mother (Commander Ballard's wife) was Madame Paling, the opera singer from Australia.

I was going home on one weekend off, up to Lemington and I was travelling on the Flying Scotsman when I met my husband to be, although we didn't get married until July 1956.

By the time the Land Army was finishing I went to work at Bray in Surrey where I was cow-keeping. I then went on to Holyport to help Major Martinborough with his Guernsey cows. He was an ice-skating judge. There was a misunderstanding while I was there so I left.

I went to work for a Mr and Mrs White at Tame in Oxford. Mrs White's sister and I became the 'milkers' and things went very well. Their son wanted more sheep and we were taking them to the field one day, him at the front and me at the back with a stick when a car comes up behind and the sheep scattered when he beeped. I got mad and on the second beep his son went to the car and sitting in the back seat were Laurence Olivier and Vivien Leigh!

Soon after that I received a message from my Mum to say she couldn't manage at home, my brother was ill and I was needed to help"

Note. Elsie left the Land Army in April 1950 after 4 years service. Elsie has received her Medal of Recognition.

Eden Hostel

67

Beetroot for Breakfast!

Elsie (Frosty) Wright nee Jackson of Donington

Iris Noor nee Eaton   Mablethorpe, Lincolnshire

I have always enjoyed a trip to the seaside but on this occasion I had to visit two ladies – **Iris Noor** and **Ethel Cannon** from Skegness who had been land girls so I had to forego my fish and chips and candy floss. It was worth it though as I met two delightful ladies who told me their stories.

The first thing Iris said to me was "I think I know you, you're face is familiar". We had a short conversation and established that years ago Iris used to live on Waldeck Road, Carrington in Nottingham. This was at a time when I was the local policeman in that area and here we were, many many years later, meeting up again. I can't remember whether Iris behaved herself or not, and she wouldn't tell me!

Iris continued, "When I lived in Carrington I worked at the Nottingham General Hospital (now demolished).I was sixteen and I saw a poster advertising the Women's Land Army. I was impressed and volunteered and was accepted very quickly. Very soon after volunteering a big parcel arrived by horse and dray delivery, it was my uniform together with a train ticket to Cleethorpes.

I went to the farm of J K Measures and we were always potato picking and when we went on weekend leave we were allowed to take 1cwt of potatoes – free. We were out picking one day when German fighter planes came over with some bombers. Bombs started dropping everywhere and we all made a dive under a tunnel, everywhere was shaking, I think they were after Grimsby. We went back to the house on the seafront afterwards to find it had gone, bombed, three land girls, the land lady and a dog were killed.

Another time we were weighing up potatoes and we were using them big weighing scales in the field. I was carrying a 1cwt bag of potatoes when the whistle blew, that was a warning of danger. I saw the fighter come over and I swear I could see the German's face. I dropped the bag and dived under the scales for cover as he turned his machine guns on us.

Five or six months later I went to Bassingham but I only lasted one night. We were picked up to go to the village dance where there was a problem – no drummer. I had learnt to play the drums when I was little so I agreed to play on that night. There were Army and Air Force lads there and I had a glass of lemonade near the drums. During the evening someone put something into my drink, I didn't know but when I stood up, well, I couldn't stand! I had never had a drink before and I just thought that I was ill. They put me into a truck and took me back to the hostel. I got a right dressing down from the Warden who said, "You'll be staying somewhere else in the morning, not here!" I kept apologising for being ill but I was sent to Whittlebury, a tiny village.

I liked it at Whittlebury. I got the nickname of 'Ricky' while I was there because I was always the fastest feeding the drum. I also suffered badly from working in the chaff-hole so they always left me on the stack.

One day I saw a plane coming in, it crashed on the lane so we all rushed there but we couldn't help. There were sweets and chocolate scattered all over and I saw the bodies burning. It upset me for weeks.

While we were there we played a game of football with the Army. The girls wore trousers and the Army lads wore skirts. I was the goalie. I can't remember the score but it was good fun. We also used to go down to the village forge where they mad the most beautiful doughnuts, they were really lovely.

I was the truck driver and had to take the girls to their farms. I had learnt to drive earlier in an old Rover and now I also drove the tractor – a John Deere.

One job I didn't like at all, it was horrible, was sheep dipping and once I tripped and nearly fell head-long into the dip. At another farm the farmer said to me "I've got something special for you" and showed me 5 young bullocks which he wanted me to look after.

We had some POWs working with us, the Germans were alright but I didn't like the Italians, they were always after the girls. One of them gave me a ring but I chucked it, I didn't want any of that!

We worked long days though, up at 5am, breakfast, sandwiches to make then off to the fields. In the summer we worked double summer time which meant the days were even longer. I found the evening meal always stodgy and I was a vegetarian! There were 50 – 60 girls in the hostel.

I was sent to a Mr Starsmore at a farm near Stoney Stratford where I was mainly employed in working with machinery. He owned 7 threshers and did lots of contract work and I did all the band cutting. Near Deanshanger, on Mr Starsmores farm, I was driving the tractor one day with the trailer loaded with hay. The load became dodgy and unsafe so I stopped the tractor and got off to tighten the load. I went up a ladder onto the hay and shouted to two 17 year old lads who were helping, "Don't move the tractor" They took no notice and moved it. I fell off and got a fractured scapula, fractured clavicle and injured my spine. I finished up in full plaster for quite a while. The result of all that was, that I was given a ticket back to Mansfield and had to leave the Land Army. Someone from the Agricultural Committee came to see me and gave me £50. I never bothered to claim compensation.

Oh, I forgot to tell you, I was sent to Kettering Hostel for a short time and we used to go to the local pub there. I can't remember its name but we met Jimmy Stewart and Clark Gable there. We had some lovely nights at that place" Iris joined the Land Army in 1940 and served until 1944 having to leave after her accident. She received her Medal of Recognition by post and attended the Celebration Service at Lincoln Cathedral on Sunday 25th January 2009.

Ethel Cannon nee Greenwood   Skegness, Lincolnshire

After visiting Iris North at Mablethorpe we moved on to Skegness to see Ethel Cannon. Ethel and her second husband Geoffrey live in a lovely flat overlooking a very peaceful sea-view in Skegness.
They both made us feel so welcome.

Iris started to describe her time in the Land Army by saying, "Forty girls all of whom came from Yorkshire came to the hostel at Thorny near Peterborough. It was quite busy there as all the aircraft used to fly up The Wash inland. Thorny was the first hostel in the Isle of Eley and we had wooden bunks, a wardrobe each and there was 3 coke stoves and 3 bathrooms. We were visited by Lady Denham who also came to our first dance at the end of 1942.

Buses used to come to the hostel and take us out to the various farms, later we all got bikes! One girl named Winnie, who was 38, couldn't ride, so we got her onto the bike and gave her a push to set her off. If she lost her balance and fell off she would have to walk to work because she couldn't get back on again. We worked hard on the farms, haymaking, we stacked eight stooks and we had to strip them with sickles.

The farmer was good, he would do anything for us. When we had a weekend leave he would order a private bus and release us early so that we could get more time at home.

One day the atmosphere was so heavy that we were all wet through. We told the farmer but he said we must finish the shift. We had a meeting about this and the Committee refused to surrender our clothing coupons for new clothes so we were shifted to March in Cambridgeshire. One day we were walking down the main street when 'beep, beep' and there was our farmer in a chauffeur driven car. He pulled out a paper to say how bad the weather had been that time. This must have been two years later"

Ethel went on to describe the problems they encountered when working in the fields with so many men around.

"There were so many men about that we complained that we were not going in the 'ditch' as we usually had to. The farmer said. "Hang on a minute Ethel" Then up came a tractor and trailer and on the trailer, a shed. "There you are Ethel, a portable s…house"

I remember when two black Americans came to the hostel and asked if it was a café. We said "No" but told them that there was a big place in Peterborough, about 7 miles away. They said they daren't go there so a Mrs Franklin took them home and cooked them a meal. We had never seen this sort of racial treatment before.

We used to have a Fordson tractor and I was just stuck on it and told to plough. I soon learned but I was never given any lessons. When a field needed harrowing I had to drag a horse up to the field and was told to get it back in time for dinner. I didn't relish the idea of having to drag it all the way back. I didn't have to, it dragged me!

One job we got was a smile. Once a week, one girl had to run round the fields – clapping, just to scare the crows!

We had some prisoners working with us, the Germans were beautiful but the Italians were idle.

We got up at 6.30am in the mornings ready for a 7.30am start, it was hard work but I really enjoyed the countryside. One day I was leading a horse, a big Shire when it kicked me, they kick out sort of sideways and Mr Burton, the Foreman made me get on the horse immediately so that I didn't lose my confidence.. We used to finish about 3.30pm but it was later in the summer months.

The potatoes were stored in 'pies' but they couldn't be opened until the man from the Agricultural Committee came to oversee it, we then had to sort them out, bad from good"

Ethel served with the Land Army from 1942 to 1945. Before volunteering for the Land Army she worked in a general store.

Ethel Cannon (2nd left back row) and friend Winnie? (2nd left front) at Thorney Hostel

Christmas 1942 - rear of Peterborough Town Hall - Lady Denham (5th from left front row). Ethel Cannon nee Greenwood (3rd row, 4th from the right)

Beetroot for Breakfast!

Jean Henshaw nee Daft.   Beechdale, Nottingham

I visited Jean at her home in September 2009; she is now disabled but still copes with life in a very positive manner. She is still able to drive and visits a couple of clubs regularly where she is a member. Jean lives alone but is completely self dependent.

I asked Jean when she joined the Land Army and she replied, "I was very naughty, I joined when I was only 15 and a half. I always looked older than my years when I was younger and when they found out about my age I was 18, too late! I wanted to get away from home, get a bit of freedom; my Mum was a bit of a gal! Anyway, I volunteered at St. Pauls, I think it was St. Pauls; I was living on the Green (Hyson Green, Nottingham) in a back to back on Selhurst Street. My uniform was delivered to the house and I was told to report to Ruddington (Nottinghamshire). I caught a train from the Midland Station and returned home every evening, it wasn't that far.

The first job I was put on was with about 50 other girls and we had to camouflage the ammunition magazines, they were underground so we had to prepare the land and then seed the mounds. We worked from 8am to 6pm. We had our meals in the canteen there, the men went in first then we followed. I was there for about 12 months and then moved to Farndon Ferry on the River Trent near Newark. I was billeted in the village hall and went out daily to different farms to work. I got lucky though. I stayed at Jimmy Smith's farm all the time, fetching the cows in and milking them by hand, there weren't any machines there! We had a real big bull named 'Henry the Eigth' there, and he served all the farms around and I used to have to take him. I used to take him on a rope and I'd ride my bike out to the farms so he could service the cows. He was a happy bull! When the foreman used to come to the field to get him he used to pick up a stick and he'd use it. I told him that one day the bull would have him and my God, he did. He put him in hospital for two months with back and leg injuries, he was more or less an invalid when he came out.

All our meals were taken at the village hall and we were packed out for the day. Every Saturday night we had a dance at the village hall. We used to dance to records and the airmen from Syston were invited. Sometimes we got a bus and went to the pictures in Newark. The lads would go on their bikes and bring us back on their crossbars. We did have a curfew, usually about 10.30pm but we did get concessions.

Being near Syston we saw the lads fly-out on their missions. We counted them out and we counted them back. Sometimes aircraft were missing; they were very sad occasions because we knew nearly all the lads"

Jean finished her time with the Land Army in 1943, she said, "My service did me a lot of good, I was much more self assured when I came out"

Jean went to work for the G.P.O. for a while and she continued, "Such was the self confidence I had gained that I was accepted in the Metropolitan Police and served in some of the roughest areas in London. I did love my Land Army days though".

Jean served with the Land Army from 1940 to 1943. She visited Hodsock Priory for a Remembrance Reunion for Land Girls on Wednesday 26th November 2008, which was hosted by Sir Andrew Buchanan. Jean said she had a wonderful time. She received her Medal of Recognition through the post. The only comment she made was the fact that her name was not on the citation from the Prime Minister Gordon Brown, which accompanied it.

The Collingham Five

Joan Baston, Ivy Bellamy, Violet Parnham, Kath Coxe and Marjorie Bingham.

I found this interview very hard to record. My wife and I visited Jean Baston at her home in Collingham, near Newark and she had kindly invited the four other ex. Land girls to be present. Memories flowed like water and the banter between the ladies was quite unbelievable. We had a most entertaining time, better than going to a comedy show and the hospitality shown to us was wonderful. I managed to speak with Joan for a few minutes before the arrival of the other girls.

Joan Baston nee Matthews   Collingham, Lincolnshire
"I used to work for Boots on Island Street, Nottingham before I joined up, that was bombed you know. I was living in Sneinton, (Nottingham) so it wasn't far to go to work. I was 17 when I joined up, I volunteered, and that was in 1943.

I was sent here (Collingham) where there were 40 girls at the hostel. The hostel is still there, I'll take you there later. It's used for something else now. I remember one girl there, she was engaged to a Bill Shaw, we were riddling potatoes that day and when we finished we picked a bunch of snowdrops for her. When we got back to the hostel her Mum and Dad were waiting for her to tell her that Bill had been killed.

That was a very sad story but there were many things which gave us a good laugh like the time I entered a 'red cabbage competition' at a show and won. Guess what my prize was, yes, a red cabbage!"

I asked Joan which work she had most enjoyed doing and which were her worst jobs on the farms.

She recalled, "I had a milk round using an ice cream trike, that was a good job, I enjoyed that but I think the one I hated most was fetching water when we were threshing. We had a big barrel on wheels, it was really heavy and we had to fill it and take it to the field for the threshing machine. That really was a tough job but thinking about good ones I loved dressing the horses ready for the annual Collingham Show, which was really nice.

I had a laugh though when the farmer tried to protect my modesty. Some bullocks were being castrated and I was sent away because young ladies didn't watch that kind of thing! The following week I was holding little piglets while they were being done.

We had a pretty good social life, there was the RAF and some Army lads stationed at RAF Swinderby and we were all invited to their dances and social events. I remember one girl who got herself into trouble and became pregnant. Her father was so mad he shot the dog!"

At this point we were joined by another lady and after a brief interval of introductions etc. (tea-making) I managed to speak with **Ivy Bellamy nee Hallam** who also lives in Collingham.

Although Ivy worked on the land throughout the war years she didn't join the Land Army until 1945. She served for the next 2 years then left to get married but she returned to work on the land again taking up her old role before joining the Land Army.

Ivy recalled a couple of stories, "We were doing general work around the farms here and there were lots of prisoners working here as well. One German took a shine to me; he wanted to help me when we were working. If he saw me grooming the horses he would say, "Here, let me do that". He left the area but later came back to find me but I had flitted. I lived at home in Collingham not in the hostel.

When we were threshing, the farmer's wife used to bring us tea in treacle and bean tins, not cups or mugs. When we had finished we used to put the tins under the cart wheels to flatten them so that they couldn't be used again. We did lots of jobs, milking, first by hand then later using the Alpha Lavelle machines. We used to do the bottling as well. Sprittling carrots and mucking out, we did the lot including cleaning up the yard once when the 'pots' were emptied from the upstairs windows!

Coming home late one evening we heard a coughing and thought it was Germans who had landed. It scared us to death but it was only the sheep!"

By the time we had reached this point in the conversations we had been joined by three other ladies. Each of them related stories and incidents but they came so thick and fast that I was unable to record them. This was when the hilarity really set in. We were laughing so much I doubt if I would have been able write anyway.

Violet Parnham nee Smith also lived in Collingham and joined the Land Army as she wanted to leave home and gain a little freedom. She was stationed at Collingham! She said that she had encountered no opposition to joining from her mother who only said, "Don't you bring any trouble home!"

Kath Coxe nee Storr served with the Land Army for 10 years – 1940 to 1950. Kath became a Milk Recorder. This was a job I hadn't come across before so I asked Kath what she actually did.

"I had to go round the farms to take and test milk samples for buttermilk content. I had to record the milk yield of each cow as the allocation of feed was based on the yield. I used to go round the farms on a bicycle sometimes having to travel up to 15 miles then I managed to buy an old 1932 banger for £32. but I had to pay for the petrol. I later got a motorbike.

Before I started recording I used to fetch the cows in for milking. There was one nasty bull in the field and one day I went in and there were two, I had to run to get away and I left my wellies stuck in the mud!"

The fifth member of The Collingham Five was another local lady **Marjorie Bingham nee Ball**. Marjorie also served 10 years with the Land Army from 1939 until 1949. Marjorie did move from Collingham to Bassingham and Wellingore hostels.

Marjorie said, "We used to have a curfew of 10pm when we had to be back at the hostel but we were allowed another hour if we went to church on a bike!"

NOTE. Whilst reading a copy of 'Lincolnshire Women at War' I saw a picture of a cap badge, one of only a handful of 10 year service badges awarded throughout the country. Both Kath Coxe and Marjorie Bingham had completed 10 years service but had received no award to that effect. Questioning this I wrote to Defra on their behalf and received the following reply.

The 10 year service award was something that we made to ladies for long service but it is thought that this may have been a practice specific to certain counties. It is not something that is possible to do in retrospect.

Dept. for the Environment, Food and Rural Affairs. 2.10.09
Sorry ladies!

It was lovely to meet with these five ladies from Collingham and it is easy to understand how well they would have worked together and very touching to see how those early friendships have survived over so many years.

Joan Baston nee Matthews of Collingham

Beetroot for Breakfast!

The Land Army Hostel at Collingham near Newark - 1945 (Photo credit - V Parnham)

*Violet Parnham and Anna
Sandbach at Collingham
- 1947
(Photo credit V Parnham)*

The Collingham Five - (2009)
L to R - Marjorie Bingham nee Ball, Ivy Bellamy nee Hallam, Kath Coxe nee Starr, Joan Baston
nee Matthews, Violet Parnham nee Smith (Photo John Ward)

Collingham Hostel today (2009)
(Photo John Ward)

Beetroot for Breakfast!

Joyce Truman nee Boston.   Lowdham, Nottinghamshire

Joyce lives with her disabled husband in their lovely bungalow home in the small village of Lowdham. I was made very welcome to their home while Joyce remembered some of her days in the Land Army.

"I was born in London then my family moved to Nottingham then on to Leeds for four year before moving back to Nottingham.
My grandparents and other family members were killed in a bombing raid on London.

Joyce told me that she joined the Land Army in 1942, she continued, "The minimum age of joining was 17.5 years not 18 years like the Forces. During my time I was based at the WLA Hostels at Hawksworth, Hockerton and Hoveringham. The hostel at Hockerton was just a wooden hut, there was also another hostel nearby at Calverton. The hostel at Hoveringham used to be a boy's home before the Land Army took it over in the war. There were 12 girls based there; it had three bedrooms and we slept on straw mattresses. It closed down temporarily after about 18 months or so then re-opened again with a new Warden.

Our uniform consisted of khaki coloured corduroy breeches and a green jumper. We had two sets of uniform. We also had dungaree overalls and when we were working on the haystacks we used to tie our trouser bottoms up with string to stop rats and mice running up our legs.

We would cycle out to the various farms, leaving the hostel at 7.30am. Our tasks included potato picking and then riddling them to grade them, picking sugar beet, swedes and peas, among other chores. We used to dig up the beet, lay it on its side so they were in row, then return with a knife to top them one by one gradually working along the row. The Irish farm labourers used to dig the beet up and top them all in one movement so they would be much further across the field than us as they had the quicker method! One thing I do remember was that they got jam with their sandwiches!

We also helped out at harvest time and I recall working the thresher at the Boots Company Farm at Thurgarton. The foreman had been very wary about having girls working on the farm; he had only ever had men before. He couldn't believe how hard we worked and he even thanked us. There were usually four Land Girls and two men working the thresher. There would be couple of workers on the haystack and one in the chaff-hole, which was a horrible job as you got prickly bits of chaff stuck in your clothes and down your neck.

When we got back to the hostel in the evenings there was always a hot meal for us. We ate lots of baked beans! We had a rota for the duties; two girls would wash up in the evening. That wasn't a popular chore because you missed the chance of going to the dance at 'The Elm Tree'. We each made our own packed lunch in the mornings"

The Elm Tree was a local public house situated on the River Trent at Hoveringham. It has now been converted into a Care Home.

Joyce continued, "The Elm Tree had big windows facing onto the river. There were lots of Australian airmen and I recall jiving was the new thing and we would jive to absolutely any music!

The pubs in the Southwell area stayed open half an hour longer than the Lowdham ones in the evenings as they were in different districts so there would be a mass exodus from Lowdham to Thurgarton to take advantage of the extra time".

I asked Joyce which work she enjoyed most and she replied, "Band cutting, and the worst was working in the chaff-hole"

Joyce was able to recall the names of the farmers at the various farms where she worked. "Others might remember them too" she said.   Three farms at Thurgarton   Mr Bentley, Mr Thornton and Mr Ploughwright, at Bleasby – Mr Spence and at Burton Joyce – Mr Peachy.

Finally Joyce remembered working in a field, near the airfield at Syerston. She was working with three other girls and the farmer, potato riddling when they saw a Lancaster bomber coming in, suddenly the wing nearest to them just fell off and the plane crashed and exploded. Joyce thinks the whole crew perished.

Joyce served with the Land Army for 8 years, 1942 until 1950. and has lived at five different addresses in Lowdham

Note. In a recently published book 'Nottinghamshire Air Crashes by David Needham (2008) there are two references to Lancaster aircraft crashing at or near Syerston airfield. One was in January 1943, returning from a bombing raid over Germany at 01.20 hours, actually crashed on the airfield, the other was in August 1943 at 15.31 hours when a training flight overshot the runway and came down in a field where it caught fire It could well have been the second crash that Joyce witnessed. On a happy note it is reported that there were no injuries among the crews on either occasion. See Addendum at the end of the book.

Beetroot for Breakfast!

The following photograph and text appeared in a local newspaper believed to be the Nottingham Evening Post.

Back row, from left*: Connie Ball (deceased), not known, Joyce Boston (now Truman) and Edith.* ***Front row****, Not known, Lorna Hooton, Marie and Olive Carr (now Prior)*

We'll Meet Again, I Hope.

They were tough days and the work was hard……

But for Joyce Truman and other Land Army girls in the picture – taken at the hostel they were billeted in at Hoveringham – there was always time for a laugh.

And for most of them now there are some happy memories to look back on. That's why Joyce from Lowdham is anxious to contact her pals from all those years ago.

She's hoping they'll get together again at the service of thanksgiving for the Land Army at Southwell Minster on Saturday.
The picture was taken during the winter of 1943-44

Just one more spadeful
Joyce Truman nee Boston (photo anon)

Beetroot for Breakfast!

All in a days work
Joyce Truman nee Boston (Photo anon)

Land girls from Hoveringham Hostel on parade in St Mary's Gate, Nottingham. (Photo anon)

During the war years Joyce and the others worked on many of the arable farms in the area – potato picking, sugar beet pulling, threshing and muck- spreading.

During the evenings, she and other girls would go to the former Elm Tree pub at Hoveringham where they used to play darts.

Twice a week there was a dance attended by some of the RAF personnel from the aerodrome at Syerston.

"We used to make some good friends with some of the aircrew" said Joyce, "but next time there was a dance sometimes we learned they had gone missing on a raid"

Joyce Martlew nee Bailey   Blidworth, Nottinghamshire.
I visited Joyce at her home in Blidworth, Nottinghamshire to find that she unfortunately has mobility problems and has to rely on help but there is nothing wrong with her memory. Once Joyce was in the mood her memories came flooding back.

"When the time came to choose what I wanted to do, munitions or the Land Army, I quickly decided,' she said, 'I went to the Recruiting Office in London Road, Nottingham. I had to have a medical and a week later two parcels of uniform arrived and I was in the Women's Land Army! That was in 1942 and I was 18 years old, living in Rainworth (Nottinghamshire)

I was told to report to Hoveringham Hostel at 8pm on a Sunday night. I got a train to Thurgarton and had to walk to the hostel at Hoveringham. There were about 18 girls at the hostel, 6 to a room and we used to cycle daily to the farms that weren't too far away.

There was an experimental farm at Thurgarton run by Boots the Chemists and just occasionally I got to work there.

One day we saw a British plane come down in a field in Hoveringham. We all ran down towards it to see if we could help but it was too hot and we couldn't get anywhere near it.

We seemed to live on potatoes in those days. Cheese and paste for sandwiches and one girl got a kipper from somewhere; she cooked it and took it out in her sandwich box the next day!

I had to do most jobs around the farms, looking after chickens, cattle, did the milking, took the sheep to the fields and worked in the fields as well. It was really hard work. I always enjoyed cutting the bands when we were threshing, you know, cutting the bands and feeding the drum. I stayed at Hoveringham for about two years then moved to Clipstone.

Beetroot for Breakfast!

'Down on the Farm'
Unknown with Joyce Martlew nee Bailey
(Photograph - J Martlew)

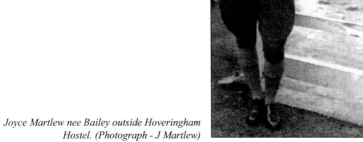

Joyce Martlew nee Bailey outside Hoveringham
Hostel. (Photograph - J Martlew)

(Nottinghamshire)

I didn't get any actual training I just learnt as we went along. Perhaps that's the best way, learning on the job because we had to do just about everything including driving the tractor. I remember one morning when I was in the boot room trying to put on my gum boots and finding a nest of newly born little pink mice in them.

All in all I really enjoyed my time in the Land Army it made me more positive and self assured. There were many highlights but the best was meeting the Queen Mother at a re-union at Birmingham after I had finished my time. I left in 1947 to get married and went back to shop work. I felt restricted and smothered for quite a long time, you know, after working outside all the time.

You asked me if I would do it all again, yes I would"

June Stoneybridge nee Bacon   Lincoln.

My wife and I went to see June at her home near Lincoln. June's daughter Elizabeth was with her during the course of the visit. June is 92 years old having been born in Doncaster in 1917, she is very spritely and still has a sharp memory. June was employed as an office worker when she decided to volunteer for the Land Army in 1943 on reaching the age of 26. She had originally volunteered for the regular Army but waited for a time and heard nothing from them. Undeterred 3 months later she volunteered again, still no reply. so she went for the Land Army.

"I was sent to Thorne near Doncaster for training and on the first night I got there the farmer wanted me to milk the cows! Well, he brought the cows in and I managed to scare the first one so I didn't get any milk. The farmer just said, "Oh, go on, get off!" That was that!

I lived in the farmhouse and went out into the fields each day; there were two lads, the farmer and another land girl who did all the driving. I remember one of the lads tried to kiss the girl and she threw a spanner at him".

I asked June if she went to live in a hostel and she said, "I was sent to Hampshire in the Winchester area to a hostel and I had to bike to a farm which was in the middle of nowhere, not just there but other farms as well. Work was being done on the Bluebell Lane at the time, you know the Bluebell railway, and we worked on the cross-beds, levelling them off. The lady there was an American and she used to help us. There were 7 or 8 working farms around there. I remember at one place, they gave us a cup on the end of a stick to put rat bait down. We did that for a couple of days and then had to go back after four days to pick up the dead rats. One day we were working in the field as usual and I needed to go, you know! Well there wasn't any toilets just hedge and ditches, so off I went. I stood up and was just squaring up my clothes, you know, when loads of camouflaged soldiers stood up all around me!

Another time we were just going back when we heard voices that seem to come from a haystack, we thought that either Germans or POWs were nearby although we couldn't see them. We had both German and Italian POWS working on the farms. Anyhow, the local police were called and they found a hidden door in the haystack and inside there were some men who had been slaughtering farm animals and selling them.

We were waiting in the yard one day, waiting to go out to the fields when the sirens sounded and overhead came a Dornier, dropping bombs. We all dived for cover but three or four people were killed in the High Street. We saw a great number of night flights passing over. There was an American place nearby and we used to do a night watch – a fire watch for 2 shillings (10p) a night".

Fieldwork somewhere in England with a Fordson Standard tractor (Photograph courtesy of Farming and Machinery Magazine)

Asked about the actual farm work they did June said, "The best job was thatching the stacks, I loved doing that. The worst job for me was looking after a horse. A man did the job really and I only helped but he had to go away. I'd only helped him for a week or so and when he had gone they said to me 'Your horse, you look after him'; I had only really held the horse for him. I had to put all the tack on him, he was very big and I just couldn't manage him. There was one kind man there and he helped me, he had a horse of his own, but this horse had a mind of its own. Eventually we managed to get him into a cart loaded with tack for the shepherd. I got it to him and he unloaded it while I had a rest; that was after three cars had scared the horse on a steep hill, I just couldn't control it. I later discovered that no woman had ever controlled that horse so the kind man took over. The next day I was told to take it to be shod, the farmer's two daughters had refused to do it, so did I – along the road for six miles? " No" I said. The farmer said, "Do as you're told" but I still refused so I was put to work in a field cutting some big yellow flowers, I don't remember what they were. While I was working a man asked me what time it was and the farmer gave me a right ticking off for talking and wasting time. I was absolutely fed up with this kind of treatment and told him to stuff the fieldwork, the horse and the job!"

I never did find out what happened after that but one can guess. June stayed in the Land Army until 1946 – a total of 3 and a half years service. June's fiancé Hubert had been taken POW in North Africa whilst laying an airstrip with the Royal Engineers. He spent 3 and a half years in Italy then taken to Germany. June and Hubert were married in 1945.

Marion Bossons nee Fuller   Rainworth, Nottinghamshire

Like all the other ex. Land girls I have spoken with, Marion was very friendly and outgoing. She remembered her service days fondly and spoke freely.

"Where shall I begin? I was 17 and a half and working for Frames, a hosiery factory in Mansfield. I volunteered for the Land Army and was sent to a purpose built hostel Mill Hill at Bingham (Nottinghamshire) there were about forty girls there and we did all sorts of work on the many farms about there. Life as okay and one day was pretty much like any other but we had times when there were plenty of laughs and the not so good days especially when the weather was bad.

One day we were working – corn stacking and the girl on the stack shouted "I'm slipping" and she did, straight off the stack and into the cart, she was okay though.

After I had been at Mill Hill for about two years I was moved to Whatton (Nottinghamshire), again it was just routine farm work but I had a similar experience to the girl on the corn-stack. I was on the cart when I slipped while we were going through a gate; I slipped off the cart and got stuck between the cart and the gate post. Like lots of other girls we used to cycle from the hostel to the farms but in the bad weather the drivers from Hoveringham Gravels used to give us a lift in their lorries. We worked with some Italian prisoners and they were okay they used to help with all the jobs. We did threshing using the old steam driven machines.

One of the jobs I had was to look after the pigs and one of them, a big old saddle-back was a bit awkward. The farmer told me to take a stick and hit him on the snout if he gave me any trouble but I finished up twisting my knee trying to keep out of his way.

Generally I liked what I did in the Land Army, it gave me a sense of belonging and that I was doing something really worthwhile".

Marion seemed to play down the work she did saying that it was like any other girl who had joined but without the commitment such as Marion gave the country would have been in dire straits.

"Have you seen the horseshoe pile at Scarrington?" she asked me, I replied that I had, "Well, she said, I even contributed to that"

The horse-shoe pile at Scarrington, Nottinghamshire is 17 feet high with a base circumference of 19 feet it contains approx. 50,000 used horse shoes and a weight estimated at 10 tons.

Joan Eggleston nee Bailey   Blidworth, Nottinghamshire

Joan still lives in the middle of farming land not far from **Marion Bossons and Joyce Martlew** although aware of each other, I do not believe they actually knew of each other prior to my visiting them.

Joan joined the Land Army in 1944 and went for a months training at the Reese Heath Agricultural College in Nantwich, Cheshire. Joan was one of the few that I had encountered that had received any actual 'pre-job' training, most of the girls learnt 'on the job'

Joan continues her story, "It was at the College that I met my friend **Lucy Moore (nee Nadin).** I was 19 when I joined up and Lucy and I were posted to Repton (Nottinghamshire) where we lived in a hostel and were taken out every day to work on the farms. After a while, Lucy and I were billeted at one of the farms and lived with a young farmer and his family. We used to do all the farm jobs – mucking out and plenty of field work and in the spring and summer, planting potatoes, hoeing, singling out the sugar beet and at harvest time, stooking the corn.

Being near an airfield at Burnaston, it's now the Toyota Factory, the RAF would fetch us land girls to their dances.

I got married the following March, the war ended in May, and I came out of the Land Army in the Autumn, my husband had been abroad. I have always kept in touch with Lucy and I still visit her.

2008 was a very special year for all of us with the badge etc. (the Badge of Recognition). My family took me and Lucy to see the farm where we had worked but it was no longer there but I remember the cedar tree at the bottom of the drive leading to the farm and that is still there.

Joan Eggleston nee Bailey
(Photograph - J Eggleston)

I had many very happy days and memories of those days and fortunately I have many photographs to look back on and remember".

Margaret Parrott nee Oldham. Penryn, Cornwall

Margaret is my wife's elder sister and has lived in Cornwall for the past 12 years. Originally from Arnold, Nottingham, she joined the Land Army and worked at Sutton-cum-Lound in North Nottinghamshire with **Jean Shirley nee Knighton and Joyce Kent nee Charlton**. Having lost touch with each other I'm pleased to say they have been re-united.

"I started work with the Land Army at Hill Farm, Sutton-cum-Lound, near Retford, North Nottinghamshire. I didn't join until 1946 after the war had finished. The Land Army actually finished in 1950 but I stayed on working on the farm for a few years afterwards. I had been living in a hostel. I can't remember its name, but there were about 40 to 50 girls there. I was moved to Bingham later.

We didn't get any training but we soon learnt what to do and lots of the work was just daily routine. I hated threshing because we girls always got the dirty job of clearing the chaff-hole and the men worked on the threshers. The chaff got everywhere, it was so itchy and scratchy especially the barley. We had one German POW working with us and he was a bit nasty, not very friendly at all. He lived in the 'big house' – that's the farm house, so one night we filled his boots with chaff, he was none too pleased!

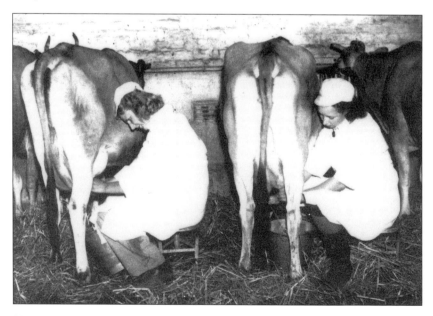

Margaret Parrott (on the right) in the milking sheds at Sutton-cum-Lound, Nottinghamshire

There wasn't a great deal to do and we worked long hours, especially at harvest time. I remember the highlight of the week was when the fish and chip van called at the farm.

Every year there was an agricultural show held somewhere near Bingham and my favourite time was preparing the Shire horses for the Show. Cleaning, combing and brushing the horses was great and then dressing them with ribbons and brasses. I remember one year winning 'Second Best in Show'

Looking back at my time in the Land Army it was good, I enjoyed it. and I was rather sorry to leave and take up an ordinary job again".

Laura Sharpe nee Shaw.   Stapleford, Lincolnshire
Laura was no stranger to farm work having been born in 1928 into a farming family who worked Strelley Farm, Strelley, just north of Nottingham. The farm was rented from a Miss Edge of Strelley Hall who owned much of the land and property in the village.

I asked Laura if she stayed on the farm after leaving school, she replied, "I had always done jobs around the farm for as long as I remember.

I left school at the age of 14 and got a job working in an office, not very exciting. I was going to work one morning, it was a beautiful day and I heard the sound of agricultural machinery starting up and I decided there and then that I really wanted to work on the land. I went to the office and handed in my notice!

My father then employed me on the land where I had been brought up, he was very strict and I felt that he tried to break me but he didn't. He didn't pay me either, oh, I got my keep, food and any clothes I needed but no pay as such, he did give me 2/6d a week (12.5p) for myself but that wasn't really pay!

We had a land girl working on the farm, my brother's girlfriend, **Pauline Hooley**, she used to talk to me about the Land Army and that influenced me and I decided to join, I was 16 and a half years old. I volunteered at Lowdham Grange, which is now a prison and later collected my uniform from the same place. The only part of my uniform I ever wore was the greatcoat and the overalls; I'd got all my own working clothes. I think I must have been the only land girl who never wore the uniform!"

I asked Laura if she was ever posted and she said, "I worked for my father just as I had been doing but the Land Army now paid me and my father had to pay the Land Army back for my work" Did your father let you keep the pay? I asked. "Well, yes but when I used to go into Nottingham he would ask me to buy seed and things from the seed merchants but he never paid me back for it. All the time I was in the Land Army I never saw anyone from the Agricultural Committee, no one ever visited to see if I was alright or anything.

I found the German POWs very arrogant on the whole but three parts of that could have been my fault, I kept myself to myself. We also had Italians and Ukrainian prisoners. The Italians were very clean; they cooked a lot in the fields. They made bread and cakes and took them to the dairy to bake. We only had two Ukrainians, one of them. Stephen was killed in a road accident outside St. Barnabas Cathedral in Nottingham

During the season we had children from a school in Kimberley come potato picking but I still did all sorts of jobs, hand milking and threshing the old way. I remember one time, after hay making we didn't finish until 11.45pm; I was so tired I slept on the hay stack all night! Talking of hay stacks, I told you my father was a stickler so early one summer evening I took my book and looked for a place to hide away for a rest and a read. I climbed up the ladder to a hay stack and settled down. A little later my father came along so I laid low. When I had finished reading I went to go down the ladder but it had vanished. He had taken it. He didn't know I was on the stack, I can imagine what he would have said had he have known. Anyway, I got down using the stack cloth rope.

I later did some work on a farm at Edingley, near Newark. We were bringing in the sheaves one evening and I was on the trailer. The load wasn't roped. We approached a railway bridge over the farm track and I could see the load wouldn't go under it so I threw off a few sheaves and promptly disappeared down a hole between the other sheaves. Richard Watts, the farmer feared the worst and was immediately sick but all was well, I hadn't been knocked off by the bridge"

Note. Laura served in the Land Army from 1944 until 1948. Richard Watts was the man who kindly introduced me to Laura and he is the Archivist for the British Agricultural Archive Film Unit. He still lives and works on the farm at Edingley.

Hilda Morley nee Spencer.   **Woodthorpe, Nottingham**

Hilda was born in Southsea, Hampshire and received her formal education there terminating at a grammar school and boarding school at Bridport. When the war broke out in 1939 Hilda was 17 years old and wanted to join the Women's Land Army as she dearly wanted to work with horses. Not being quite old enough she took a part time job working in a restaurant.

On reaching the age of 17 and a half Hilda volunteered for service with the Land Army at the recruiting centre at Lee-on-Solent.

Hilda took up the story, "I didn't get any formal training and I was sent to Colonel House's farm at Crofton near Stubbington where I mainly worked in the dairy. Colonel House had a herd of 40 to 50 head and it was a tough job milking the cows by hand, I just learnt the work as it came along. I think it was all that hand milking that gave me rheumatism eventually, that and stripping the sprouts in winter! This was at a time when they were just introducing milking machines on the farm, the cows didn't like them at first they used to kick out but they soon got used to them."

I asked Hilda where she was billeted and she replied, "I was in a cottage near Stubbington, it was the head cowman's cottage, there was no electricity, no hot water. I had to boil a little water to get a bath, it was never really hot and I had to bathe out back of the cottage.

Later I went to work in the big field looking after the chickens. There was about 2,500 to 3,000 Rhode Island Reds, we had incubators, we had everything, a complete chicken farm. Then, one night there was an air raid and everything went, all the chickens, the incubators everything was destroyed."

I asked Hilda if Colonel House started the farm off again after losing everything, "No" she said, "I went on a milk round, it was a big round, so much so that I finished up with a four wheeled cart for the deliveries. I remember one particular day, I used to stop at a crescent of houses with a sort of lynch gate in the middle, an entry into a field. I used to stop there and count up the milk deliveries to work out if I could give a little extra to those who asked because milk was rationed you see. Well, this day I was aware of a plane buzzing about fairly low, I didn't take too much notice as planes were always flying about so near the sea then suddenly it came in again, really low this time and the horse took fright and bolted. I was sat on the cart but I didn't have a hold on the reins but I managed to control the horse and we stopped a little way off. I had heard a crash and turning

I saw that the plane had crashed by the lynch gate right where we had been standing. I swear that that horse saved my life by bolting like that. I found out later that the plane was a German recognisance plane.

Another thing I well remember was the day when an American Officer asked if I would like a trip to see the Solent Lightship, there was three American Officers billeted nearby. I said, "Yes I would like to go, so he took me – by canoe!"

Later in her service Hilda asked for a transfer and moved to Nottingham, to Poley's Farm at Arnold, that was in 1946/47 and only remained there for a few months as she married in 1947 and returned to Southsea.

Hilda is a lovely lady with a very sharp mind and a wonderful memory, she has lived in Woodthorpe now for many years. She received her Badge of Recognition after serving a total of 8 years in the Land Army and in closing Hilda said, "Some of my happiest days was in the Land Army".

Hilda Morley nee Spencer (centre) still showing winning ways with her local bowling team

Sylvia Hatcliffe nee Hough. (Deceased)   **Stoke Bardolf, Notts.**
Jessie Chisnell nee Stone.   **Sutton in Ashfield, Notts.**

I received a message to say that Sylvia Hatcliffe's daughter may be able to tell me a little about her mother's service with the Land Army whilst stationed at Stoke Bardolf, Nottinghamshire. I visited Mary Hatcliffe at her home in Stoke Bardolf which is a small village situated on the Banks of the River Trent.

Mary told me that her mother was born in Arnold in 1915 and left school at the age of 14 to work for Allen & Solly, Hosiery manufacturers of Arnold.

In 1939 Sylvia joined the Women's Land Army and worked for a while at Poley's Farm in Arnold carrying out general farming duties before being sent to the Bingham Hostel. It was whilst at this hostel she met with another land girl **Jessie Stone** (now Chisnell) and they became firm friends. They received no training before they were sent off to work at Stoke Bardolf.

I later went to see Jessie at her home in Sutton in Ashfield. Jessie said her memory wasn't very good so I managed to ask a few questions in an effort to help her remember.

Jessie said, "When we arrived in Stoke Bardolf we were sent off to find our own digs, it was only a tiny village and I went to a Mr and Mrs Lounds, who were very good. I had my own room but there was no hot water in the house. Sylvia went to stay with the Mallyons".

Sylvia's daughter Mary came with me to visit Jessie, as they have been friends all these years and Mary reminded Jessie of the work she and her mother carried out on the sludge beds of the Estate. The Estate was the property of the Nottingham Corporation Developments and the girls working there were required to clock on and off every day when reporting for work. The time clock they used is now on show at the Industrial Museum at Wollaton Park, Nottingham.

Jessie joined the Land Army at the age of 18, signing on at the local Labour Exchange and was sent direct to Bingham. I asked her about her time before she joined up and she said, I was at school in Sutton in Ashfield until I was 14 and left to work at Edgar Slack's Knitwear until it was time to join the Land Army. I chose the Land Army because I loved being outdoors and I wanted to stay near home and, like I said, they sent me to Bingham. I remember it was a Wednesday when I went to Bingham and I was home again on the Saturday for a weekend." Jessie continued, "We did all the usual farm-work including milking the cows but we had a milking machine on the farm. I used to love fetching the cows in .and taking them back along the Trent side.(River).. It was so peaceful and sometimes I used to take a book with me".

I asked Jessie about the food she received and she replied, "The food at the billet was alright but the sandwiches were horrible though, always cheese or fish paste"

Asked about social events, Jessie said, "We used to go to the pictures at Carlton, the Old Ritz cinema, its gone now. And we used to go to the dances at Gedling Memorial Hall. We used to go on our bikes".

There were other girls working on the Estate but two other good friends appear to have been **Winnifred (Winnie) Scott nee Wall** and **Norah Wardle.** Both Winnie Scott and Sylvia Hatcliffe stayed on to marry local men and live in the village. Sylvia went to live at Top Farm with husband Harry who was resident Stockman.

I also asked Jessie what she liked most about farming and she replied, "Taking the cows for a walk as I said" And the worst? "Oh, threshing, we used to thresh using the old steam engines. I do remember once though, when we were loading up a cart with sheaves, I was on the cart when the horse bolted. Bounce, its name was, it ran the full length of the field then onto a path outside the field and took me back to the house. It frightened me to death it did".

We had some prisoners of war working on the Estate some Italians and one Austrian who took a shine to me. I enjoyed my time in the Land Army, I had a sense of freedom and doing something worthwhile even though there was a war on".

Sylvia Hatcliffe nee Hough passed away in 2007 aged 92.

Norah Wardle never married and passed away in 2006.

Winnie Scott nee Wall now resides in a Care Home on Carlton Hill, Nottingham.

Jessie Chisnell nee Stone still lives in Sutton in Ashfield. She received her Badge of Recognition and attended a reunion at Hodsock Priory.

Note. Mary Rose Hatcliffe has written a 32 page booklet on 'A history of Stoke Bardolf' which contains 3 or 4 interesting farming photographs and information on the area.

Farming in the past at Stoke Bardolf

Harvesting in the days of steam
Photograph by Robin Stone (deceased)

Steel lugged wheeled tractor at work at Stoke Farm at Stoke Bardolf
Photograph by Robin Stone (deceased)

Note - *Robin Stone managed Stoke Farm during the war, he also represented Stoke Bardolf on Basford Rural Council*

101

Beetroot for Breakfast!

Sylvia Hatcliffe nee Hough

L to R Charlie Morley, Sylvia Hatcliffe nee Hough, Jessie Chisnell nee Stone, Albert Morley, (kneeling) Winnie Scott nee Wall, Norah Wardle - 1942

LETTERS

A number of letters have been received from ex. Land Girls who live too far away for me to visit or they preferred to write of their experiences.

(These letters have not been altered in any way other than to hide the exact addresses of the senders for security purposes.)

Beetroot for Breakfast!

Miriam Haigh nee Barr. Milton Keynes

Dear Sir,

"My niece sent me your letter to 'Inside Lincolnshire' knowing that I had been in the WLA in Lincolnshire for one year during the war.

When I was 17 in 1941 I applied to join the WLA. I was at that time in Yorkshire, the eldest of five children. My father was a railwayman, mother busy with her children and two evacuees. I was sent my uniform and a railway voucher for Sutterton with Algerkirk in Lincolnshire. I would be met at the station there by the farmer.

Monday morning in February, cold and damp, two trains both of them late. It was war-time! Met by the farmer, a man in his 30's, a bit put out by my lateness as the cows needed milking and his wife didn't milk, neither did I, but I jolly soon learned. Five cows, all in milk, four quite easy, but one, oh dear, first time calver didn't appreciate a first time milker.

The farm that I had arrived at was a smallholding of 37 acres (I think), run by the farmer, his wife, (ducks and chickens), a youngish lad in charge of two horses and myself, (very green but quite willing to learn) The holding was about a mile from the village of Sutterton, midway between Boston and Spalding, one of an original 150 acres. The farmer's wife was a kindly soul who was, I think, rather pleased to have another female around. The farmer, a very hard worker himself, expected the same from everyone else. The lad thought himself the bee's knees and rather despised the townie who knew nothing!!

Tuesday morning, after milking, then breakfast, fat cold bacon, bread, jam. I ate the bread and jam, but I'm afraid I wasn't much on fat bacon which rather threw the Mrs as that was the only meal around just then. Anyway, we then went up the lane to the potato grave which we opened up and started to put up the potatoes after riddling them into a hopper to fill sacks, quite a feat I can tell you, anyway I learned. All that week that was the job in hand, putting up spuds to take to the station on Saturday morning.

We didn't go by any clock, just the trains running by. Lunch was taken by the 11.10 called 'pudding' because that is what we had, in some parts of Lincolnshire the first course of dinner was pudding, usually steamed apple or other fruit, suet pudding with custard, very filling, so you didn't want much meat and veg. afterwards. It actually suited me as the meat was once again fat bacon.. Then back to work again until milking time, mucking out etc. It was jolly hard work but I seemed to think I had to do it so I got on with it, gradually getting into the swing of it and I did enjoy the milking as I got to sit down and be able to sing to the cows, much to the amusement of the Boss and the lad, who couldn't sing a note anyway.

Saturday was an experience. After milking I was having breakfast and the Boss explained that the lad and I were going to the station about two and a half miles away with the potatoes we had put up that week. The lad was getting the horses ready, the boss explained that Shirley, one of the horses, was a bit spritely but the lad would have her and I would have Prince as he was much steadier. Just then, through the window I saw the horse, a great big one on its hind legs with the lad just holding on. I said, 'Is that Shirley?' The Boss said, 'No, that's Prince, he's a bit frisky as they haven't been working for a day or two. You imagine how I felt but we settled down and I quite enjoyed getting off the farm and seeing where I was.

I stayed at the farm for a year and went through the whole farming cycle. We put up all the potatoes, the sugar beet plants were thinned by hoes and then by hand, separated to one plant, back aching work., potatoes set, another back aching job – thank goodness for milking. I could sit and sing to my cows. Hay making, not a lot of that as most of the land was arable and every last foot of it was ploughed – a one furrow plough turning one furrow back along the edges.

The Boss was very good in his way to me, but of his language, something his poor wife apologised for but I didn't think he thought about it at all.

We had the excitement of pig killing time. We kept two pigs which we were allowed to kill as part of our bacon and lard ration. I helped the Mrs at that time as there was such a lot of meat to sort out, pies to make, sausages, haslet, pig fries to make up for the neighbours. We never killed pigs together, everybody did it separately so that there wasn't a glut of meat. Sharing it out meant there was quite a bit extra at times.

A lot of farm work was tedious and jolly hard work, in the fine weather most enjoyable but in the rain, oh dear. I blame my present rheumatism for that! I did enjoy the harvest but the extra hour meant we were working late getting the yields onto the carts so we could unload them in the morning whist the dew was still on the corn in the fields. Potato picking, we didn't do much of that as the Boss got a local gang to do most of it. Wouldn't let me work with them as his wife said they were too coarse! He really was a kind man in his way and protected me from a lot. When the cows came into season he had his wife explain what it was all about. Poor man didn't like to explain himself.

The whole time I was at the farm I never had anyone from the WLA ask me how I was doing or anything which now, on thinking about it, I find rather odd. I had every Saturday afternoon and Sunday off so I was able to make friends in the village. The locals were quite amused about me at first but they soon got used to me and found that ignorant as I was I soon learnt.

I had the Christmas off and went home to find that my mother wasn't at all well so I decided I ought to get nearer home and was allowed to go back to Yorkshire and started working in the North Riding.

Oh, I didn't have to exist on fat bacon in Lincolnshire as the Mrs boiled a shoulder of ham for me which the lad didn't think was fair but I enjoyed it very much. I did, in time, enjoy a bit of fat!

I hope you find these reminiscences useful

Yours faithfully
Miriam Haigh

Note. Miriam left the Land Army on 27th December 1945 after four years service. She received her Badge of Recognition form the Lord Lieutenant of Buckinghamshire at Bletchley. The ceremony was held upstairs at the T A Centre and there were several young men present to assist the ladies with the stairs if required as the lift had broken. Miriam was asked if she needed assistance and her daughter, who accompanied her, replied that her mother was quite capable. "I could have hit her" said Miriam. (Do they ever change?)

Sheila Wilkey (nee unknown)   Spalding, Lincolnshire

Dear Mr Ward
"I joined the Land Army and was stationed in a hostel in Waltham, nearest town, Grimsby. I made some very good friends from all parts of Britain, myself from London.

We did find the work very hard and were very stiff and aching when we arrived back in the evening, having to slide on our bottoms on the polished floor as we couldn't stand we were so stiff. That was the first week. After that we got used to the weeding, sowing, picking apples, life became more enjoyable.

Sometimes we cycled to work but if it was far away we had one girl, a

driver, who used to take us by lorry.

Lovely bunch of girls, we all seemed to like the country but did get homesick sometimes. The RAF used to come into the Hall and we would put music on and have a dance. Then they would send a coach and pick us up and take us to their place where they had a big room for dancing. So life did have some good times.

I would love to hear from anyone who remembers Waltham Hostel run by a Miss Spencer. My single name was Sheila Wilkey and I do remember many girls' names who worked with me

I left Millwall, east end of London and I have heard that a very close neighbour lives in Lincolnshire. Her name is Sheila Wing and I would love to hear from her. I knew about the bombs , we were in the thick of it. The thought of the war still makes me feel how lucky we were to have survived as many we knew did not. I left London 25 years ago and now live in Lincolnshire.

Sorry for not cutting things short but I could go on about the lovely people who lived in Millwall. Good luck with your book, I wish you every success"
Sheila from Spalding.

A Plea from Sheila who would dearly love to find her old friend again, she is thought to be living in Lincolnshire.

Pat Ingram nee Trickett.   Tasmania, Australia.

I was very pleased to receive a letter from Tasmania in July 2009 which goes to show how the ex. Land Girls have settled around the world and how they are still in touch with others who spread the news and uphold many life-long friendships. I wonder just how far some people have travelled and settled since leaving the Land Army?
Dear Mr Ward,

"I am ex WLA and still correspond with one of my colleagues at Collingham near Newark and in her last letter to me, she enclosed a cutting of your request in a newspaper for experiences etc. of ex WLA so I wish you good luck with your book. I spent 3 years in the LA so I will try and tell you of my experiences and I must tell you at the beginning they were some of the happiest days of my life.

During the war years at 17 years of age you had to register and either go into the forces or at munitions. As I was under age, my father would not sign for me to go into one of the forces and I did hanker for the LA, always loving the outdoors and nature.. Therefore on May 26ᵗʰ, 1943 after my 17ᵗʰ birthday I joined the WLA and was sent to a hostel at Sutton-on-Trent for a months training. I was assigned to a farm walking through the village daily. I was taught to milk a cow and to work in the fields. After the March I was sent to live in at a farm in Plumtree. I only spent two months there , I was lonely although well looked after. The farmer's wife used to make tarts from the milk when a cow had just calved and it was lovely, just like thick custard There was a body of ladies who dealt with our welfare and I requested to be moved to be with other girls. On 1ˢᵗ August 1943 I was sent to Collingham just outside Newark to a hostel run by the Y.M.C.A. There were four of us in the carriage going to Collingham, one was Joan (Baston, whom I still correspond with. Joan still lives in Collingham, she married a farmer, she's now a widow.

There would be about 45 of us, 4 to a cubicle. We were all issued with bicycles and some rode for miles to their farm. We had a 'forewoman' still in LA who saw to our time sheets and sent us to the farms where required. I used to dread threshing, a filthy job, you ended up looking like a chimney sweep at the end of the day. If I remember correctly there was one shower and about four baths so you used to have to wait your turn and clean it afterwards.

I was lucky and spent a lot of time with one farmer. Frank Shaw of Collingham. Frank taught me to plough with his two huge horses, 'Kit and Dick' I used to plough some acreage near the main railway lines going to Lincoln from Nottingham. The travelling servicemen would whistle and cheer me. Frank and I would empty the crew-yard (manure), he would have a horse and cart and so would I and we would go and flick forkfuls over the paddock, the horse plodding very slowly, ploughed it in later.

At the hostel we were woken at 6am, wash, dress and have breakfast. There would be slices of bread, beetroots, cheese, paste etc. we would prepare and pack our own lunch... A good hot dinner would be waiting for us after your wash out back and change of clothes... There was a roster for us to do the dishes, wash and dry at nights and we would have a film show periodically and a dance monthly where we would invite the local army and air force to join us and supper afterwards.. We all went home of a weekend to Nottingham but you had to be prepared to work overtime sometimes till 8.30pm or 9pm when hay making or harvesting. There were plenty of laughs, 15 to 20 of us were sent to a farm, I can't remember what for, threshing or carroting and the farmer's wife stood there to greet us with her elderly father in pyjamas and as we passed the elderly gent exposed himself (nothing to see!). One or two of us giggled and passed some remark and the farmer's wife said, "Pay no heed, he is showing off"

Frank, my farmer, had geese in a paddock up on a hill and I used to love to cycle with a small bag of corn and climb over a sty, lift a latch and let them out. As we walked to the hut I left a trail of corn, I would lift the latch and run like billy-oh, the old gander would flap his wings and screech and chase me... Then, once over the sty, I had to count them as so called gypsies were camped nearby.

Winter was the worst, carting in thick frost and snow. I recall cycling with the front of my hair peeping out of my pixie hood and eye lashes frozen and had like icicles hanging. We used to love a wet day, really pouring; we would have the day off.

It was only last year Mr Ward when the WLA was finally recognised for our efforts. 62 years after me leaving I received a badge of honour and a letter from our Prime Minister Gordon Brown thanking us for our efforts. I am 83 and a lot of ladies would have passed on and missed out.

Whilst at Collingham I started writing to an airman who was in the Middle East, he was in the same squad as one of my LA friend's cousin. We wrote regularly to each other for over a year. Fred was overseas for 4 and a half years, he came from Plymouth. Meanwhile I left Collingham and was still in the LA I went to live with my sister, now 93, at Carlton Hill, (Nottingham), her husband was overseas. I did a year cycling daily to Mapperley to Wickes Market Garden (now Florilands) on Catfoot Lane.

If wet I went by bus that too was very interesting working in the vast greenhouses with tomatoes, lettuce and flowers, as Mr Wickes had a stall in Nottingham Market.

Meanwhile Fred came home from overseas and looked me up and within six months we were engaged and Married. Fred will soon be 88 and still driving and active. We have had 63 years of good happy marriage and three children, five grand-children and nine great grand-children.

We came out here in 1965 for a better life and found it. Tasmania is an island of about 502 thousand, all colours and creeds here now. The climate is very much like England, we have gales, snow and ice, it's very hilly and mountainous. Fred and I came home for a visit in 1975, we

Beetroot for Breakfast!

found England had deteriorated but it's still home!

Sorry I cannot send you any photographs of myself in LA uniform; my grand daughter has them all, she has compiled a family tree. I have found one of us all outside the hostel in 1945 and our pet lamb. I am the end one on the right, second row up, hands in pockets. Joan, who I correspond with is 3rd from left, top row, our Forewoman is sitting on the ground, out Warden is holding the lamb.

Must close, wrist and fingers aching. Hoping I have been of help,
Best of Luck
    I remain
        Yours sincerely
            Pat Ingram nee Trickett.

PS. When going home on leave Frank would pack me eggs, chicken and home made butter, a real treat. Frank was middle aged and he married Cynthia, sitting in front of me, both passed on now.

The girls outside the YMCA Collingham Hostel, Lincolnshire 1945 Pat Ingram is on the right, second row up

Pat Ingram nee Trickett who now lives in Tasmania

Pat Ingram nee Trickett and friend in Newark Park - 1945 (below)

Beetroot for Breakfast!

Eileen Summerfield nee Touson   Spalding, Lincolnshire

Another letter received tells how much life in the Land Army was enjoyed
by the vast majority of girls who left home to work on the land'
Mrs Eileen Summerfield writes

To Mr Ward
*"I joined the Land Army in 1942, leaving my lovely city – Nottingham. I
was sent to Spalding where I met another girl, Mrs Pole of Astly. We were
met by the farmer who took us to our billet – the foreman's house.*

*We worked from 7am till 4.30pm, cycling to the fields with our packed
lunch. We picked strawberries, did hoeing and weeding the crops and in
the fruit season we had such long ladders to pick the plums and apples as
the trees were so high.*

*One hard job was spraying the fruit trees in the winter with a white
oil spray and in the spring a yellow spray. We held a long rod which
connected to a tank on wheels through a long rubber tube which was so
heavy to hold.*

*I loved every moment of the life as it was so different to city life and I
learned how hard it was for country people.*

*I was pleased to receive my Badge of Recognition and proud of it. I'm
also quite pleased that you are intending to write a book about the brave
girls who tackled these very hard jobs.*

Yours sincerely
Mrs Eileen Summerfield.

P.S. I was born at Basford and went to Scotland Road School. I am now
88 years old and my friend Mrs Pole and I still keep in touch since 1942.

Marjorie Curtis nee Nixon.   Birchwood, Lincoln

I received Marjorie's letter at the end of August 2009 and from her letter and others I have received I have been quite surprised at the diverse duties undertaken by the girls although much of the work appears to be of a very monotonous nature.

Dear Mr Ward
I have only just seen your letter in the County News regarding ex. Land Army girls and their lives during the war.

I stayed in Lincolnshire for three years, first at Cuxwold than at Bransby. Whilst at Cuxwold I did have an unusual experience for a young girl of 19 years, being marooned by an enormous snow-storm.

I was billeted four miles from the poultry farm where my duties were, together with the other land girl Eva, to care for about 500 birds each. The birds were hatched from the incubators on the premises and after a few weeks, hopefully in the spring weather, the chicks were put outside in small shelters called arks.

On a cold, dark Sunday morning I started to cycle to work when it began to snow. Very gently large flakes floated down and before I was half way there I had to dismount and push through six inches of snow. Arriving was a real struggle, the cycle wheels were solid discs of white and my boots heavy blocks of snow. The Manager and Eva had set up the original shelter and were trying to rescue the tiny chicks as they foundered in the snow. It was hard work as ones clothes soon became heavy with snow which was now a blizzard. Both lanes out of the village were four feet deep in snow almost to the hedge tops. Eva was billeted at the Manager's house so it was decided that I would share her room. We were all very tired so after borrowing soap and a towel I slept in my undies.

First job next day was to shovel our way out to see how the birds had survived. With bright sun and brilliant blue sky we were in a winter wonderland. Icicles hung at great length from roof, gates and ledges. The wire netting between the chicken pens was solid with melting snow glimmering like diamonds. The good weather lasted for about four days causing the picturesque scenery to slowly melt away until life was back to normal.

After four days without a change of clothes or toiletries, the lanes, at last opened up again and I was able to cycle back to my lodgings after a

most scary country adventure, just so the nation could have an occasional egg!!

All this seems such a long time ago but I hope you gather enough for a small article for your book.

Yours sincerely

Marjorie Curtis (Mrs)

Note. There was no fixed ration for eggs but the allowance was one egg per ration book when available but often it was one egg every two weeks.

Dried egg was available – one packet every four weeks – a packet contained the equivalent of 12 eggs.

Barbara Elliott nee Pearson (deceased)   Warsop, Nottinghamshire
I have received a letter from Mrs Marian Asher of Warsop, Nottinghamshire, who wrote to tell me of her sister Barbara Elliott who passed away on 25th March 2008. Marian sent an interesting and lengthy letter which is reproduced in full.

Dear Mr Ward

Further to your letter in this weeks issue (19 July 2009) of the 'Chad' newspaper regarding the work of the Land girls and Timber Jills during WWII. I thought that I would forward these few details which I recall relating to the time my sister spent in the Land Army in case it might be of use to you.

My sister, Mrs Barbara Elliott, regrettably died on 25th March 2008 just a few weeks before she received her WLA badge/pin for which I applied on her behalf as she was ill and we knew that she would not get better. I really wanted her to receive it.

Barbara was born in 1923 (Barbara Pearson) in Warsop. When she was 18 years of age and knew she would be 'called up', she was working at Mansfield Shoe Company. I think she felt that she would prefer the outdoor life instead of the other services and she volunteered, with another work colleague, for work in the Women's Land Army. Her friend's name was Lillian (Lily) Redmile. Both girls were sent to work in Buckinghamshire and they were billeted in the village of Cuddington, a few miles from Aylesbury, at a house called 'Rose Tree Cottage' with an extremely kind and good elderly couple, Mr and Mrs Tom Clark (or Clarke). As an additional little point of interest, just across the road in the village, the Dimbleby family were staying during the war thinking it would be safer for Mrs Dimbleby and her children while the well-known Richard Dimbleby was away in the Forces or on some kind of war work. Jonathan wouldn't yet be born but little David Dimbleby would wait for the land girls arriving home from their work on the land and beg for a 'piggy-back'.

Mrs Clark, who was very good to Barbara was a wise hard-working woman, had a saying (a kind if mantra) "There's no such word as can't!" That stuck with Barbara all her life and she was very tenacious and persevering when beset with life's problems all life long. There was not any running water in the cottage and all water had to be drawn from a well outside and on winter mornings very often the ice on the well had to be broken first... Also there was no electricity and they had to rely on oil lamps and possibly candles.

Later on they had to move to 'Friarage Camp' which I believe was in or near Aylesbury, and which housed many land girls. Barbara said that it was not unusual to hear rats scurrying around at night (not good for someone afraid of spiders!). Also another disturbance and worry for them at night was at a time when the German V2 rockets were raining down on London, sometimes they either fell short or over ran the capital and would drop in Bucks. When the sound of the cut-out and silence came they often ran out into he night in their pyjamas hoping and praying that it would not land and explode anywhere near them. Fortunately they remained safe.

Barbara's hand was badly injured during her service in the WLA. It was at harvest time and her left hand was caught in either the threshing machine or the binder – I am not entirely certain which and I don't wish to mis-lead you in this respect. For a while it was quite serious and her thumb was just pulp but in the end some kind of thumb was restored to her although it was badly misshapen and lost some of its function.

As they worked the farms near certain aerodromes it was not unusual for German planes to fly overhead, probably getting the airfields in their sights, especially Halton.

Barbara always said that she worked on the land with numerous Italian Prisoners of War (POWs) It seems that one of these prisoners was very much like Charlie Chaplin, both in appearance and gait, so the land girls nicknamed him 'Charlie' which made him rather cross as he thought it must be a derogatory remark, which of course, it wasn't. They got on well with the POWs.

When the girls could arrange any kind of party by saving up their food rations and sweet ration coupons – they did. I believe Barbara's 21st birthday party was just such a party. The girls would wheel some of the injured airmen and soldiers to share in it. Stoke Manderville Hospital was near and the renowned Archie McIndoe was doing revolutionary pioneering work on severely burned airmen and furthered the skin grafting techniques. Also I believe that at Barbara's 21st party some members of the Free French arrived to share in the already meagre fare – their food and sweet rations had been saved up a long time for the party.

Eventually part of my sisters work involved collecting various types of agricultural machinery and taking it to farms all around Buckinghamshire.

*It was all housed in a central depot, possibly Bletchley, but I am not certain. Everything was geared to keeping the country fed and making every possible use of the daylight hours and then there was double summertime, the clocks being put forward then for two hours (not one as now) The seas were so heavily mined that the merchant ships couldn't get through to bring food and goods and so with the men being away at war the land girls did **much** to keep the nation going. Without them it could have been a different story!*

To finish on an amusing note, one morning Barbara and another land girl were sent off very early to collect a flock of sheep from a railway station a few miles away and drive them back, on foot, along the country roads, again several miles. They were inexperienced in dealing with flocks of sheep and the sheep had minds of their own and would stray off the country roads and try to get into the fields – if one strayed, they all strayed!! I think it turned into quite a pantomime and those very weary land girls collapsed exhausted into their beds that night, as they still had their other tasks to perform. My sister never saw sheep in quite the same way again – although she loved them, - she never forgot that episode.

Another point that comes to mind before closing. whenever Barbara had any leave she would always try to get home if only for the weekend. Often she could only get as far as Nottingham before the last train had gone and would sleep on the station until there was a train for Mansfield the next morning. Alternatively she would hitch a lift home from lorry drivers etc. (something a girl could not safely do now) and always was treated with the utmost respect and kindness. There seemed to be a very different spirit then – everyone pulling the same way and helping each other the tragedy which is war.

None of this may be of any help whatsoever to you, Mr Ward, but I could not ignore your letter in the local paper and felt honour bound to report what little I know of that time. I hope that you will glean much more information from the remaining land girls who can tell you more fully about the work they did for their country.

Yours most sincerely
(Mrs) Marian Asher.

Beetroot for Breakfast!

Derek Twells   Stamford, Lincolnshire

I have received an unusual letter which was written by a man who has memories of land girls working on his father's farm. The letter is mainly of interest as the girl's names are not known but the article may stir a memory or two for someone. I reproduce Derek's letter in full.

Dear John

Ref our telephone conversation yesterday I enclose my less than exciting Land Army photos. As you can see these are very much working examples taken on the spur of the moment.

I am aged about two so it would date them as 1943. Obviously it's winter time as the trees are bare and we are all well wrapped up.

The little white dog was called Micky and lived to be 16 years old. My father who was the farmer is in the middle of the group with hat and my mother is shown wearing a 'pinney'.

The young lady kneeling down holding a hoe (with me) is quite distinctive looking, so she might be recognised by grandchildren.

The place is Ewerby Thorpe near Ewerby, north of Heckington and due east of Sleaford (4 miles approx,) It would be interesting to know where these girls were based.

Best wishes, sincerely

Derek Twells.

P.S. My father's name was Thomas Henry Twells, known as 'Harry' My mother was Sarah. My parents were at Ewerby Thorpe throughout the war years.

See photographs - is there anyone you can recognise?

A young Derek Twells with his Land Grls on his father's farm c1943

119

Beatrice Babura (nee unknown.)   Connellsville, PA.
A Letter from America
I was extremely pleased to receive the following letter from Beatrice who
lives in Connellsville. Philadelphia and I wondered just how far afield
some of the ex. land girls have settled.

Dear Sir
*I was born and raised in Carlton a suburb of Nottingham, a town made
famous by Robin Hood and his Merry Men. Whether he was real or just a
legend he sure was responsible for bringing in thousands of visitors.*

*I left school at fourteen, the mandatory leaving age at that time and
was soon working in an office for Boots Pure Drug Company.*

*When war broke out I wanted to join the Royal Navy but my father
wouldn't sign for me so I volunteered for the Women's Land Army. I was
soon on my way with another local girl, to a small village by the name of
Swineshead, close to Boston, Lincolnshire. We planted, hoed and picked
the mature potatoes and did the same with the beans. Once the season
was over we were assigned to a place in Northampton, we didn't fit in there
at all and when we went home for a weekend, we never went back. This
didn't sit well with the people in charge. We had a serious meeting then*

went off to a Hostel in Orlingbury, close to Kettering, Northamptonshire and we found our niche there. The work was very hard, much different to my 'cushy' job sitting at an adding machine but all made acceptable by the good friends, several of which I myself have kept in touch with over these many long years.

We just took over the men's work who were off in the different services keeping us safe. We threshed the corn, wheat, which was a very hard and dirty job. In the winter's cold weather I found it hard to keep my hands and feet warm but just 'soldiered on' making the best of it.

We worked with many German and Italian prisoners, we never feared them, and they weren't responsible for finding themselves in such dire situations. One Italian by the name of Remo would regale us with jokes told in his broken English, that would keep us laughing and make the day pass quickly. To this day I often think of him and wonder how he is doing after he made it home. He was one pleasant fellow.

One night, a girl from the Hostel and I were at a dance at the YMCA in Kettering when we met two American airmen, Francis Joseph Babura and his friend Tony. I won! Oh course, we two girls missed the last bus (9pm) back to the Hostel, so the two guys walked us back all along those country lanes and then in turn they had to walk back to their barracks. This was the start of something good for me, we became an item and I took him home to meet my parents on my 21st birthday and he was a complete hit, especially with Granddad Daykin (my Mum's Dad), he was an old soldier and had a fetish for cleanly shined shoes and since Frank was always clean and neat down to his shoes, he won old Granddad's favor.

We were married in Carlton at the Catholic Church 'Sacred Heart' and Frank had to get permission, as I was Protestant and I had to promise that all future offspring would be raised Catholic. I left Nottingham on 12th April 1946 for instruction at Tidworth, southern England. I was soon on the Swedish liner M.S. John Ericson for a nine day voyage but I never once got sea-sick, just a little queasy as we hit the New Jersey shoreline. Then a train ride to Connellsville where I was met by Frankie and his friend Ted Owens and I was soon on my way to meet the in-laws and enter into a whole new life style. Years later I learned that the M.S. Ericson was burned up in New York harbor.

I had three children, two girls and a boy, all grown, working and have their own families. I did turn Catholic when my first daughter was a year old and they all went to Catholic school and are true to the faith.

Beetroot for Breakfast!

I think that's about all for now, except to tell you that after almost forty nine years of happy marriage, I was made a widow fifteen year ago. My husband was diagnosed in England with Mitral Stenosis and told he would have problems later. He under went two open heart surgeries in the VA hospital in Oakland, Pittsburgh, a very trying time for all of us. He came back fine, only to succumb on 26th May 1994 in the same hospital. He was cremated and we had a Mass for him in St. John's Here in Connellsville and the remains are laid to rest in St. John's cemetery and that will be my final resting place.

I wish you luck in your endeavour, a worthy cause.

We did get a Land Army and Timber Corps badge and a letter from Gordon Brown M.P. current Prime Minister, thanking us, a little late, but welcome anyway.

Sincerely
Beatrice.

I think it is evident from Beatrice's narrative and certain spellings that she has been in America for a very long time. It is good to hear how life after the 'Army' has been for her. I have recently received another letter from her mainly to tell me how her family are keeping, sending her seasonal greetings (Christmas) and enclosing the photograph of herself in uniform together with her friend.

Beatrice Babura (right) and her friend Joyce Calladine (left)

122

Audrey Murden nee Greaves   Kirkby in Ashfield, Nottinghamshire
Another article from a man comes from Barry Greaves. I visited Barry
at his home in Kirby in Ashfield and he later furnished me with the
following story of his sister (now deceased) together with a number of
extremely interesting photographs.

*Audrey entered the Land Army service in 1945 at the age of 20 and
was posted to a billet at Gringley on the Hill, north Notts. near Bawtry.
Sometime during 1946 she was moved to Hawksworth, a small village
near Bingham in Nottinghamshire. She was to remain at Hawksworth
until she left the service to get married in December 1947.*

*Little remains of the Gringley Hostel which was on West Wells Lane
in Gringley. After it was closed as a hostel for the Land Army personnel
it became a Borstal and then a Detention Centre site. It is now (2009)
waiting to be developed as a residential site. It also appears that there are
no local residents of Gringley that served in the Land Army.*

*In Hawksworth Audrey was billeted in a hostel that was a large house
adjacent to the church and appropriately it was called 'The Rectory'
(not to be confused with 'The Old Rectory' WLA Hostel in Halesworth,
Suffolk – the subject of Irene Grimwood's book 'Land Girls at the Old
Rectory')*

*It was thought by one of her former colleagues at Hawksworth that
she had been asked to move because she had been disciplined for staying
out in the evening later than she should. But this is only rumour and I
do not know the exact details. Before the house was used as a hostel for
the girls, it did house soldiers but what their purpose was in a village of
that size I do not know. At Hawksworth, Audrey worked on various farms
around the village including those owned by the Burtons and the Buxton
family. The normal working week was five and a half days (55 hours) and
the girls that could not go home for the weekend had to pay something
towards their board and lodging for the extra one and a half days that
they had to say in the hostel. There were 32 girls housed at the hostel in 4
rooms, each one having 8 bunk beds. The girls soon forget their modesty
as the washing and bathing was a very communal affair. Elsie Burton,
one of the girls there recalled going to the bathroom for the first time.
She was given directions, as it was quite a distance from the bedrooms
(dormitory) she was assigned to. She recalls opening the bathroom door
and finding one girl on the toilet, one at the washbasin and two in the
bath. She quickly closed the door and fled back to her room but she was*

soon to get used to it.

The girls came from different parts of the country. Some like Audrey and her friend Carly Leatherland lived relatively close as did Margaret Monks from Pinxton (see page 31) But there were other girls like Elsie Burton (Burton being her married name) who along with three other girls came from London.

When Elsie travelled to Hawksworth for the first time she met two other girls at the railway station and all they knew was the name of the place where the hostel was situated and that they had to catch a train to Nottingham. On reaching Nottingham they then found that there was very few people who had heard of the village of Hawksworth and even less knew how to get there. Eventually they were directed to the correct bus which took them to the village of Whatton. From there they then had to walk more than 3 miles along dark lanes. To make it more difficult, because of the conflict there was no road signs, these had all been removed. Quite an ordeal for a 17 year old girl. The fourth girl who should have been with them and who had missed the train then had to do the same trip but all on her own. Even more of an ordeal!

The Hawksworth Hostel opened in 1943 and closed in 1949. The girls worked on all aspects of farm work from ploughing to tractor driving and land reclaimation. They started work at 7am and cycled to the various farms. After work and 'play' the doors were locked at 10pm.

Audrey served in the Land Army from 1945 to 1947 and sadly passed away in October 2004. It is lucky that she left many photographs of her service days and these are greatly cherished by her brother and the family.

I am indebted to Barry for contacting me with this valuable piece of Land Army history in Hawksworth.

Audrey Greaves

Haymaking Time at Gringley on the Hill - 1945

Beetroot for Breakfast!

Audrey Greaves and Joan Davies - 1946

Reunion of girls from Hawksworth Hostel (at original billet) - April 2009

Mary Smith nee Firth.   Louth, Lincolnshire

In response to my letter of appeal in the 'Inside Lincolnshire' paper, I received a reply from Corrine Smith who told me that her Nan, Mary Firth had written down her duties and experiences whilst she served in the Land Army. Mary, who is now 85 years old, still retains her great sense of humour. Here is Mary's account as I received it.

Dear Mr Ward,

It was in April 1941 that I decided that I ought to do something to aid the war effort. I was almost 19 and in a comfortable job as a short hand typist, living with parents on the outskirts of Nottingham. I had lived a very sheltered life – arriving rather late in my parent's life. All our pleasures and activities were found within the chapel and I belonged to the chapel youth club. My attention had been drawn towards the posters advertising the Women's Land Army – a picture of a young girl – tanned – hair blowing in a gentle breeze and yielding a hay fork. That, I decided was the life for me – a complete change from the routine of office work. After filling in the enrolment form I was summoned for an interview where I was told that girls were urgently needed for milking and dairy work. I was much too shy to say that wasn't exactly what I had in mind. I would be given a months training.

I had never been near a cow in my life, viewing them only from a railway carriage en route to our summer holiday and occasionally seeing them in distant fields on a visit to the countryside. I was very dubious regarding the difference between a cow and a bull! Certainly I couldn't ask anyone – those things just weren't discussed in those days.

About a couple of months later my uniform arrived – by post. Jodhpurs, blouses, jumpers, great coat and a hat, with dungarees, boots and wellies for working. The instructions said I was to report to a farm in Torksey in Lincolnshire where I would receive my months training. There were several more new W.L.A. recruits waiting on Nottingham station, but not one of them was the so called urgently needed milk girls. They were all going to a hostel and would be sent out daily to work in the fields as and when required by local farmers. They were full of high spirits and were aghast when I told them what I would be doing. I arrived at my destination to find another land girl – Christine and we were both being billeted with the farmer and his wife for the month. It was a large farm with two dairy herds and each month they trained two girls – one to do the hand milking and the other machine. Before I could open my mouth my new found friend seized the opportunity to announce she would do machine milking. I felt she had a decided advantage over me, living just a few miles away.

My first shock came with a visit to the outside loo – I thought all homes in the British Isles had flush toilets. I was horrified to find an old earth closet, nor was there a bathroom – only a sink and an old pump in the kitchen. That evening a terrible home sickness swept over me....What had I done? My visions of tossing hay in the summer sun had faded and I felt trapped and doomed. I was to report to the cow stable at 6.30am, a time of day that had previously never existed for me. I carried my candle upstairs to bed – the cottage only had electricity downstairs, clinging to the hope that in some miraculous way the war would be over in the morning, peace would be declared and I would go running home to my nice modern home and comfortable life.

6.30am arrived and the war was still on and after a quick cup of tea I walked along to the cow stable, a long building where about 20 cows were tied – it was lit by hurricane lamps and I found the smell revolting.

Two men had already made a start on the milking and one of them introduced me to my 'practice' cow. Apparently all the girls learnt on that old cow. He sat down and gave me a hurried demonstration, issuing a few instructions and left me to go back to his milking, saying I would soon get the hang of it! He had showed me the art of holding the bucket between my legs but my knees were shaking so much I couldn't keep it there. My mouth was parched and I felt sick with fear. My mind began to wander as I sat there. I thought of the number of times I had been taken by my parents to the pantomime in Nottingham – how everyone had laughed when Idle Jack had tried to milk the cow by pumping its tail up and down. I thought, sitting there, that it wasn't all that funny – just a jolly good idea. How I wished that was the way things were done. I hadn't really taken in what the cowman had said. Was it the back two first? Then again, he could have said the front two first. Would the cow object if I took them in the wrong order? Perhaps it was one from the front and one from the back. The possibilities seemed endless. Was it rather like bell-ringing? If you took things in the wrong order, everything fell apart! The cow was still munching at her food and it seemed the sensible thing to do was to get the job over before she realised what was happening at the other end! I leaned my head against the cow, stretched out my arm and felt around. Was there just four? The whole operation seemed positively disgusting to me. It just didn't seem to be the decent thing to be doing

– groping around under that cow. Had he said a squeeze and a pull or a pull and a squeeze? I was just about to make a start when something nearly rocked me off my stool. I had never thought that cows coughed and thinking I was about to be attacked, I fled with my bucket and stood with my back flattened against the cow stable wall, shaking with fear. I could hear the milk swishing into the buckets at the other end and the two men laughing and talking as they milked. There was no way out for me – I'd just made my bed and I'd jolly well got to lie on it. I plucked up courage and went back extracting about enough milk to make a cup of tea. The awful thing was that it wasn't just a one off thing, it had got to be repeated every morning and afternoon for heaven knows how long. My confidence gradually increased and by the end of the month I was milking my practice cow and one more. The cowman wasn't at all impressed – it seemed the previous girl had been milking six cows by the time she left.

My new posting instructions arrived at the end of the month. I was to go to North Somercotes on the Lincolnshire coast where I would be employed in milking and general farm work. I was to live in the farm house with the widowed lady farmer. On my arrival, the first thing I noticed was the open copy of 'The Christian Herald' on the kitchen table, and one of the first questions she asked was – "Do you go to chapel?" "Oh yes, I said – and we take the Christian Herald at home". Well, this seemed to clinch it – I was it seemed, the answer to a widow's prayer. Over a cup of tea she told me that her farm worker and herself had not attempted to unpack the newly installed milking machines, but thought it advisable to await my arrival seeing that I had been instructed in the art of machine milking and therefore knew all about it. It was when she began enquiring the make of the machine I had been using that I had to break the news to her that I had never handled a machine. It seemed that the WLA Authorities had blundered – Christine had been sent to where they did hand milking. It was when I went to the toilet that I decided that at all costs I must master those milking machines – the toilet had a chain! I felt quite heady with relief! There was no toilet paper – after all there were shortages of most things, but there, in a wooden box was an old Methodist hymn book. I thought it was carrying things a bit too far – Christian Herald on the kitchen table, Methodist hymn book in the toilet. I assumed she had taken the hard covers off before she put it there! I shall always remember – she was up to the Christmas carol section when I arrived – No 130 – 'It came upon a Midnight Clear'. I was quite sorry when we reached the index at the back of the book.

Beetroot for Breakfast!

There was electricity upstairs and a tap over the kitchen sink – one of the most modern houses in the village she told me. Between the three of us we mastered the machines and I was duly left in charge of the milking. My courage and expertise grew and a quiet understanding developed between me and the cows.

On my second morning, I met Sam, an old bearded man who helped out at busy times. He was waiting for me in the yard, engrossed in lighting his pipe. Without looking up he shouted at me in the broadest Lincolnshire dialect – "Fetch bee-ast from cloo-as". I didn't understand a word of it – so I said in a nice polite voice "Pardon" hoping to get it the second time around. Without looking up he said exactly the same thing. I just wondered what my next move should be, when he glared at me and shouted "Are yar dee-af – doo-ant yar speak English? The cloo-as, it seemed was the grass field. Apparently all the fields in Lincolnshire were called 'close'. However, I thought what I lacked in knowledge I would make up for in willingness. I opened the gate and tore down the field and the cows scattered in all directions. It took a long time before Sam accepted me.

My lady farmer also kept pigs. The pig house was a long low building – a narrow passage down the side with five pig stys and I was sent to clean them out. No-one ever gave me any advice regarding the right way to tackle the job. It was a case of trial and error. The pigs were being fed kale. Long thick stalks – the pigs ate the leaves, gnawed at the stalks and then left them. They were lying in disarray in the pig muck. I couldn't balance them on my shovel and if I pierced them with my muck fork, they wouldn't come off. I began to grow desperate – I had still a list of jobs to do and it seemed the only way to deal with those stalks was to man-handle them. They wouldn't balance on the wheelbarrow, there just wasn't enough room for me, the barrow and the kale stalks so I picked them up, one in each hand and carried them out to the muck hill. The mess I got into was unbelievable. The little pigs ran between my legs, my nice clean dungarees were absolutely lathered up. Each morning I climbed into a pair of dungarees stiff with a mixture of pig swill and cow and pig muck. I had pig potatoes to cook outside in a large steamer. Now, there is nothing tastier than a newly cooked pig potato. I would sit on the meal bin and munch a couple, feeling rather like the prodigal son – 'and he fain would fill his belly with the food that the swine did eat'.

I am a very mild tempered person and I find it very difficult to explain what happened to the chickens. I had instructions to clean them out – the hut was in the farm yard – no deep litter or battery hens in those days. My lady farmer had gone to Louth and it was my first attempt at mucking out the chickens. I flung the door open, convinced that I could manage the chickens better than I did the pigs. They were young chicks – about six weeks old, and I think they must have heard about my inexperience, for as soon as I opened the door – out they started to fly. I slammed the door to keep the remaining ones in and went after the culprits. My only implement was a shovel so I kept trying to pin them down with that, but I must have been rather heavy handed because I laid them out, - I knocked them unconscious! I was horrified. What explanation could I give my lady farmer? I would clean the chicken hut out first and then decide but a few minutes later the chickens started to come round and whilst they were only still half conscious and staggering around, I grabbed them and flung them back into the hut.

In the 3 and a half years I spent in the W.L.A. I tackled all types of farm work. My love of the countryside grew and I count my time amongst the happiest of my life and I never did return to town life.

Note. I never intended to comment on any of the letters sent to me but I felt that I had to publish this letter in full to show the wonderful sense of humour possessed by most of the ex. land girls I have encountered.
Footnote. On 28th January 2010 I received an email message to inform me that Mary Smith nee Firth had sadly passed away last December.

Beetroot for Breakfast!

Marjorie Nix nee Cromer.   Runcorn, Cheshire.

The next letter was received from Marjorie Nix together with a small presentation made by her niece Wendy Brownlow who was aged 14 years when she produced it, some 40 odd years ago!

Dear Mr Ward

I have a relation who lives near Grantham, she sent me a cutting from the paper about you wanting to know about the Land Army. I really fancied the Land Army and couldn't wait for my 18ᵗʰ birthday. So the week I was 18 I joined up, that was in 1947.

I was sent to a Hostel in a village called Bassingham, about 10 miles from Lincoln. We were all new so we didn't know anyone, but I soon found a pal and we kept in touch for about 40 years. I was a bridesmaid at her Wedding, and she had several holidays at my house with Jim and me. She died a few years ago.

I was born in Widnes, Cheshire which is between Liverpool and Manchester. Jim and I retired from Wollaton near Nottingham, to Derbyshire, which is a really lovely county. Sadly Jim died six years ago and I came back to Cheshire to be near family.

I hope this letter will be of interest to you and readers. There is a lot of stories and things I could tell you both good and bad but its too much to write about as I have got arthritis quite bad, so John I hope you can read my letter writing. I am now 81 years old – not bad for an old girl eh?
Mrs Marjorie Nix

A second letter was received at the same time.
John,
My niece did the enclosed paper at school; it may interest you and your readers.

One day, Jim and I had a ride out to Lincolnshire to see if the Hostel (Bassingham) was still there, they had changed it and now it's the village school. We had a ride to Ponton near Grantham to see that Hostel, that is now bungalows for pensioners! A lady came out and I told her that I had been a Land girl there and Surprise, Surprise; she had been a Land Girl and was sent to that hostel. She married a local boy and got one of the bungalows when the L.A. finished. She was there when the WAR was on. Once again I'll say, Good Luck John.
Marge "Butter" Nix.
PS. My maiden name was Cromer just case someone may remember me.

The following is a transcript of the presentation (word for word) made by Marjorie's niece many years ago.

MEMORIES OF A LAND GIRL

'In the winter of 1947, at the age of 18, my Auntie Marge joined the Women's Land Army. She was posted to a village 10 miles from Lincoln.

There was 50 girls living in hostel, they slept in bunk beds in one long dormitory. Before going to bed every night they had to pack their sandwiches for work the next day, 6 slices of bread and butter, 2 slices of meat, cheese or jam, to put on the bread. They each got a tin to put the food in, to keep the mice and crawlies out while they were in the fields, the farmers used to bring a cup of tea to them usually in a bucket, they went out of the hostel at 7.30am and got back at 5pm. 1947 was the biggest snowfall England had for years all the land girls were sent to dig the village out, the snow was 4 foot deep. Things got better as Summer came, doing all the different jobs on all the different farms, they always went to work in lorries, and coming back from work, they all sang at the top of their voices a song they made up called, GIRLS OF THE LAND. Aunty Marge still sings that song. A lot of the farms had German prisoners, 2 land girls to 1 German, you had to work together. The older POWs were alright, but the younger ones, no one liked them, they acted like Nazis, a school is now where the hostel was, Auntie Marge and all the girls got moved to Grantham in Lincolnshire, to another hostel. She remembers picking potatoes and they kept finding money, the farmer said he always let the fair use that field, a gang of girls went to work for one farmer who told them to hoe a huge field of sunflowers, they thought it would be a lovely job working in a big field full of flowers. The excitement didn't last long when they saw the tiny little 5 inch plants. Being townies, the girls forgot plants start from seeds and didn't know the season for flowering, one of the worst jobs was picking sprouts, they were covered in thick ice, all the girls were fed up and very cold and wet, some of them wondered why they had ever joined up in the first place, the river was quite near the hostel, after tea in summer they used to swim, the hard work was soon forgotten. The nearby R.A.F. camp would send a couple of lorries for the girls to go to the dance. The dance was the highlight of the week. 12 land girls including my Auntie, went to a farm weeding a field of onions. It was at this farm she met the farmers son, who is my Uncle Jim.'

Beetroot for Breakfast!

Mavis Maltby nee Morley. (Deceased)   Sherwood, Nottingham
This letter appeared in a newspaper, possibly the Nottingham Evening
Post, but it was sent to me by Mavis Maltby's daughter Jean Taylor of
Arnold.

*'My mother Mavis Maltby went in the Land Army at the age of 15. She
was based at Coddington, near Newark*

*She loved being on the farm and would tell us about helping to bring
the cows in for milking and watching the lambs being born, also rearing
some of the runts on bottles.*

*Mother was going home one weekend and times were hard, so when she
was offered a cheap rabbit to take with her she was over the moon. She
couldn't wait for her mum, "Grandma Edna" to see the contents of the
sack. What a shock when the sack was opened. It contained a hare. She
knew a rabbit from a hare a mile away after that experience.*

*Although mum was young, the Land Army was wonderful. She was
living at Dakeyne Street off Carlton Road and knew the sadness of the
war such as the tragedy of the Dakeyne Street air raid shelter. She and
her sisters had run home quickly otherwise they may have been in the
shelter. My granddad and Uncle Frank helped with clearing some of the
rubble. The sight was to remain in the memory for a lifetime.*

*I enclose a poem based on a lot of things mum and dad used to say.
Waste not want not is still a favourite saying. Wartime people would go
mad if they saw the contents of today's wheelie bins!*
Jean Taylor

Note. Jean's poem may be seen in the 'Poems and Pieces' chapter at the
end of this book.

Joan Dunlop nee Bennett. Toowoomba, Australia.

I was delighted to receive a letter card from Joan who lives in Toowoomba, Queensland. Our land girls have really settled far and wide but are obviously still in touch!

Dear John,

A young friend who lives in Newark sent me the article from the newspaper about the W.L.A. during the war.

I was 17 yrs old when I found myself in Collingham, Nr. Newark in 1942, in a WLA Hostel.

It was hard work for me, a Grammar School girl who had never done a hard days work but I loved it... Up early, out on the road on my bicycle with my snap tin; we sang as we singled carrots, up and down the rows endlessly, sorted potatoes in an old fashioned wooden riddle; one day we were riddling away when we heard a plane overhead obviously in trouble; we watched as something black and ominous fell from the plane and feared the worst as it plummeted into the next field. When no explosion occurred we rushed to the gate and saw a hole with a plane's engine in it, black and smoking. One of ours limping home, informed the police.

During my time at Collingham I met many people, some who correspond to this day. I had a milk round in Collingham for a farmer which I did on a tricycle with a side cart where the churns sat.

My memories of the Land Army are all good and finally I had to leave because I severed a tendon on one of my fingers, cutting bands on top of one of the old steam threshing machines. Unfortunately the old village doctor only had two remedies; some foul tasting chalky mixture for the inside and calamine lotion for the outside; my finger remains crooked to this day.

I married an officer in the R.A.A.F. stationed at Waddington, Lincs., that's why I'm here. I could actually write a book about my land army days but at 84 I can't be bothered, my memories suffice.

I'm a West Bridgford export and went to the Manning Grammar School on Gregory Boulevard. My son, Adrian, now 59 went to Arnold County High, he's here now. Hope this has helped you
Yours sincerely
Joan (Dunlop)

P.S. I was Joan Bennett in the Land Army.

Beetroot for Breakfast!

Joan sent me two newspaper cuttings taken from local papers in Queensland.

Letter of the Day
Brit's DST memories
My only experience of daylight saving was British double summer time during the war.

I was in the Land Army and it was for the benefit of farmers to enable them to harvest crops until 11pm.

I didn't as I was young, healthy and got paid overtime on top of the basic 30 shillings a week.

Leading in sheafs of corn was heavy taxing work for young girls, especially as we were missing out on our evening meal at the hostel; the farmer's wife was supposed to feed us.

All we got night after night was lettuce sandwiches and water; ugh!!

That's the only thing that stays in my mind about daylight saving.

Joan Dunlop. Toowoomba

The second cutting read:

More Giggles
This happened many years ago, not funny at the time but very amusing in retrospect. Picture the Land Army in wartime Britain and me a young naïve girl away from home. All the young ones in the hostel swooned over the handsome farm lad and he asked me out

From a big city, I went all out for the big date. Stockings painted on with pencilled seam, hair up in combs, best dress and plenty of make-up.

He arrived dressed rather casually I thought, and off we went.

Not to the local hostelry for a drink and a sing song.

To my horror he pulled a ferret out of his pocket and announced we were going rabbiting. After stumbling over ploughed fields in high heel shoes, leg tan running from light rain, hair fell down, crepe dress shrunk and clung. I looked a wreck and he didn't seem so attractive.

First date was the last date.

Joan Dunlop. Toowoomba.

Evelyn Shepperson nee Cubitt   Cropwell Butler, Nottinghamshire

I joined the Land Army in 1947 when I lived in Romford, Essex.

I was stationed in a hostel in Roydon, Herts. A very large Victorian house.

We went out in gangs, digging dykes, pulling swedes etc.

My brother married a farmer's daughter and I met her brother and we started to keep in touch.

I then applied for a transfer and was posted to Woodborough Notts, the accommodation was in Army huts, with a coal fire with a chimney out of the roof and concrete floors. Very cosy!

We went out in gangs again, picking potatoes, brussels and tying flax. I volunteered to be in charge of the library that was in the office which kept me occupied in the evenings.

There was a request for someone to go rat-catching so I volunteered to have a go, and it enabled me to learn to drive.

I was with two men and we would visit farms, lay rat feed for three days and then put poison down in the run. Any bodies we found we would remove and get rid of them.

We also used to poison moles. This was done by first digging for worms, and then chopping them up into a tin; we were then given Strychnine to mix with them.

We would then find a run, make a hole with a stick and with tweezers. drop a worm in the hole and cover it with a stone. It all sounds very Heath Robinson now but it worked.

There was no means of washing your hands, or rubber gloves, so we used to put newspaper round our sandwiches to be on the safe side!

I passed my driving test in 10 weeks.

Where there were horses we had to use poison that was safe, as horses (and rats) cannot be sick....

I finally left the Land Army in 1950 to get married, but it was a great experience. I often wonder where all the girls are now.

Hope this is interesting enough for you

It is so long ago now, (I am 83 next Birthday) and there is a lot I cannot remember....

Sincerely

Evelyn Shepperson.

Beetroot for Breakfast!

Muriel Beeston nee Brain.   Worksop, Nottinghamshire.

I was extremely pleased to receive Muriel's letter which enclosed an account of her time with the Women's Timber Corps when she was stationed at Collinbourne Forest in Wiltshire. Muriel, now 85 years old, better known to her friends as Mary still lives in Nottinghamshire and was in the Timber Corps from May 1942 until September 1945.

After meeting and talking with Doreen Hall about her life in the Timber Corps, my friend Dorothy Chilton and I decided we would volunteer for this. We were approaching 18 and a half years and would either have to go into the forces or a munitions factory. We went to Ranby for an interview and about two weeks later we had been accepted and our uniform and instructions arrived, we were to report to Weatherby for a months training there. We were shown how to use an axe, bushman's saw and cross cut saw, also to identify soft and hard woods. It was April or May and very hot we got very sunburnt and I remember not being able to sleep because we were so sore the sheets hurt. When we were asked what county we wished to work in Dorothy and I said Gloucester so we could be near Doreen – the nearest we got to this was Wiltshire and we never saw Doreen until after the war.

It was the Thursday before Whitsuntide weekend when we arrived at Ludgershall by train and were met by our new boss Mr Alec Robertson – who was about 30 years old and told us he would take us to our digs on his motor bike. I told Dot to go first and after being told which way to go I was nearly there when he came back for me – I didn't fancy riding pillion, then later on I often had a ride to work on one of the timber fella's bikes and enjoyed it.

We stayed with Mr and Mrs Andrews (this was my mother's maiden name) for 2 and a half years. The bungalow was clean and we had good food, except our sandwiches which never varied at all like Mothers Pride flour- namely Marmite on 2 slices and soapy cheese on the other 2. As you can imagine, working outdoors we were very hungry and often went scrounging around the gangs for anything they couldn't manage. One amusing incident was when we reported for work on the first Friday morning they told us that the saw mill was going to close until Tuesday after Whit. so we were told we could go home. Now we had already sent a telegram to my Dad to say where we were but instead of the post mark being Andover, it was Dover, my parents were very upset and went to tell the Chiltons. Al they could think of was that we must be loading timber at the Docks which were being bombed at that time. We arrived home after travelling all night and they were very relieved when we said we were stationed at Collingbourne Forest near Andover.

After we got back I was sent to work with two brothers who were the best Timber Fellas in the area. I had to help crosscut – very low, not like they do today – just clearing your knuckles, then when the trees were down – we lopped off the branches. The trees were then measured by the two Molly's one short and dumpy and one tall and slim. They spent their days going to different gangs of timber fells measuring and counting etc. and depending on what they could get out of the trees decided the men's pay. They always liked a good big tree the base usually went for the saw mill then probably a 9 ft. pit prop then into 6 ft. pit props and so on, the branches were trimmed and cut into cord wood which the girls did and was stacked into a cord (a measure) of wood between 2 stakes. This was collected by tractor and trailer by the girls and taken to the charcoal burners. Two Swedes ran this and depending on their drinking, operated almost every day.

Once a month we had to take turns to collect the charcoal and take it to Ludgereshall rail sidings where it was loaded and despatched somewhere. Another job we did was to saw 3 ft. pit props from smaller trees. My husband used to say that he hoped I sawed the wood better than I did the bread! My Dad told me that we sent some of the props to Whitwell pit. (near Worksop) Sometimes we were sent with a large timber lorry to fetch the trees for the saw mill, these were snagged out by girls driving tractors and then loaded up by the help of skids which we had to stand by and help roll up the trees. It was fun riding on top – dangerous I think now looking back. Then came the clearing and burning which always seemed to be in very hot weather, the branches etc. which were no use were gathered and burnt leaving the woods nice and clear.

The Silver Birch twigs were collected and bound together, trimmed and then made into besoms – brushes to clean the charcoal furnaces. On odd occasions we were sent to load pit props into wagons at the sidings- this was a bit scary but looking back I don't think at all suitable for a girl to do. We were taken into the woods in the morning and unless it rained we stayed until 4.30 – 5 o-clock depending on the distance we had to travel. If it was raining when we arrived we waited in the saw mill until it cleared up or were later sent home. If it started to rain or snow whilst at work we had to stay until 2 o-clock under a tarpaulin or what was available when the lorry would come for us. I think this contributed to my rheumatism *as I was invalided out by Dr. Evans after 2 and a half years service. Dot Chilton stayed on a few more months working in the saw mill operating a huge saw which she preferred to do rather than being in the woods. We were very brown and developed a few muscles and enjoyed it very much indeed.*

If I remember correctly our wages were 25 shillings (£1.25p) per week and our board was about that every 2 weeks. We didn't get underwear provided and had to buy all our personal things – toothpaste etc. bus fares into town, Andover once a week and Salisbury perhaps every month. We could wear civvies when we went out or uniform, 2 travel passes a year (took all day or night). My parents sent me my bike which I used to ride to the saw mill instead of waiting for the lorry. The people in the village used to ask us where we had been felling and went along with prams and handcarts to collect the chippings or spare wood which they stacked up ready for winter to burn in their homes. Dialect was strange but so was ours to them I suppose – we were a mixed bunch! We always mashed tea they always brewed or made it.

The Italian prisoners of war worked close to us and would bring us a taste of their rabbit stew which they cooked on a fire in the woods. Buses in the little villages only ran about once or twice a week. We went walking and asked for a bus home and they told us there wouldn't be one until Wednesday! We were given tinned food from the Americans which I brought home to Dad and we were allowed a bag of sugar a month and one tin of condensed milk for tea in the woods. A billycan was placed on the fire between two sticks and we were told to throw a twig into the can to stop the tea tasting of smoke.

Most people I met were 'ships that passed in the night' but good memories remain with me. I am glad that I was guided back to my church and my family. I married my husband the following year and had 56 years of happy marriage. Looking back it is only then we realise just how much we owe to early days and guidance by loving parents and God's grace to us.

We didn't receive any gratuity and had to return all our uniform. All I could keep was my Timber Corps Badge.
Muriel Beeston

Retired land girls sampling a little of the life of a Timber Jill at a reunion - location unknown. The land girl in the centre is Marie Bannister nee De Wael at the age of approximately 86 years

Beetroot for Breakfast!

Marion Goodenough nee Stokes.   Scunthorpe, Lincolnshire

Marion has taken the time and trouble to set down her memories in the very welcome form of an essay which is reproduced as written.

THE HOME FRONT, WOMENS LAND ARMY BY MRS MARION GOODENOUGH

Looking back on my Land Army days is a mixture of highs and lows enjoyment at the pleasures we made in our free time and the sheer weariness, exhaustion and sometimes boredom of the jobs we had to do.

Six of us met up on Nottingham station to travel to Swineshead in Lincolnshire. We were already good friends when we arrived, none of us knew what we were letting ourselves in for but it was an experience we will never forget.

There were sixty five girls together in a hostel, we found out in the weeks to come that the hostel had been an Italian prisoner of war camp, but the prisoners were moved because it didn't comply with P.O.W. standards.

We had only half our uniforms, no waterproofs, wellingtons or working shoes we had to manage with what we could find amongst our civvy clothes. It was mid summer and the weather was hot.

The work was horticultural rather than farming, but working all day in the hot sun our hands were torn by constant handling of vegetables which had to be topped and tailed ready for market, in some cases we had to crawl on our hands and knees to single out small plants because they didn't provide us with hoes to chop them out. At the end of the first few days we were so stiff in our limbs it was almost impossible to walk and our arms and faces were blistered with the sun we thought we had arrived in a place next to Hades.

None of us had ever been away from home before but we had volunteered and we had chosen the W.L.A. instead of the A.T.S. or the W.A.A.F. The thought of being outdoors in the fresh air and able to get a sun tan was our thought rather than the work itself, but in reality it hit us in those first few days

Potato picking was a back aching job and this wasn't helped by the local women land workers, they were used to the job but were spiteful enough to move the markers making it a longer stretch for us to cover, when the tractor came round with the spinner he just laughed and covered up those we hadn't managed to pick making us look slow and stupid.

Into autumn we realised just how bad the hostel was, we were paddling

through rain and even snow was coming through, it was so cold we were glad to go out to work to move around to get warm.

As we were about to start on the sugar beet, the powers that be the W.A.E. committee decided to move some of us. Good News, we thought, perhaps we were going to a better place but then realised that we were being split up. I was on my way to West Rudham in Norfolk, my friend Joyce was going to Kettering in Northants. It was very emotional and quite scary going off alone to another area.

This was the beginning of another phase of what the W.L.A. was all about; this was 'real' farming.

The hostel had just twenty seven girls and we went out to farms every day doing whatever work needed to be done.

Sugar beet was very hard handling, chopping and loading on to high sided lorries or carts for eight hours a day, there was never ever any thanks from the farmers, they never really wanted us but they couldn't manage without us. When we finished earlier than they expected in clearing the land they couldn't show any appreciation at all.

In the four years I served I worked with horses (nearly collared myself instead of the horse when it reared its head) I drove a tractor hauling a combined harvester (they didn't have their own mechanism in those days). Eight hours of this in the hot sun and often overtime until ten thirty pm (it was double summer time) to get the cereals in.

I was a 'shepherdess' and a 'scarecrow' when I had to rattle a tin with stones to keep the crows off the winter wheat that was just showing through the ground.

We were treated like convicts when we were made to rake up great boulders into heaps then load them to be taken away so that the field could be made ready for food; every inch of land had to be productive because the country was on the verge of starvation.

The W.A.E.C. then decided we could probably manage to do general draining; these were massive field drains which were thick with slimy weeds and gravel. The drain sides were six feet high and we stood in water over our knees, we had waders on but everywhere was covered with ice and snow. The shovels were almost too heavy to lift even before they were filled and we were throwing it over our own height.

There was never any privacy, toilets are not situated in open fields and most hedges had been chopped down for more land to be used. We found a small broken down cottage this was bliss indeed to be able to 'spend a penny' without everyone looking on.

Beetroot for Breakfast!

On the third day we found a dip in the land near to our ditch, we knew straight away that it was an unexploded bomb. I still can't understand to this day that three nineteen year old soldiers lost their lives whilst digging it out. It was in an open field, we laughed and talked with them to within half an hour of it exploding as they stood on it to dig it out, and they said they had dismantled hundreds of that type of bomb. They had no fear, but one wonders why it could not have been blown up instead of dismantled. But war was so many different things, we knew great tragedies but there was also excitement, the highs and lows of war was something we got used too.

We had a wonderful social life; there was a dance at each surrounding village every night of the week including Sundays. Cinemas at the R.A.F and Army camps. Every home in the village had a licence to sell alcohol not that we ever had more than one drink per night, it was always a social event when we met to have a chat, we did pair off and have dates but in all my four years there, there was not one girl ever in trouble or danger.

In 1944, about April time, the village was suddenly filled with hundreds of Army personnel and all manner of vehicles. They were the 'Desert Rats' and had arrived back in Britain after fighting in the Middle East for three and a half years. We soon found out that they were back to prepare for D Day. We were proud of the fact that just twenty seven girls were revered enough to be let in on the secret of the great day that was coming.

Back at work we carried on with all general farming whatever the job we did it, working with horses, tractors, combines and muck spreading there was never a day off if it rained or snowed. We picked sprouts and cut cauliflowers till we thought our fingers would drop off. When threshing time started it was all hands on deck, going from farm to farm until each one was finished, on top of a stack with nests of little pink mice round your feet or the chaff hole where little prickly bits of straw and dirt pushed through our clothes. All farmers helped each other until all was completed. When it came to lunch times they were all given a hot meal by the farmer's wife in the farm house. We were left to get on with our two slices of bread each of jam and potted paste and a flask of tea; sitting in the barn (only once in four years was I offered a cup of tea).

We had some unbearable times when we needed all the strength we could muster mentally. One of our girls lost thirteen members of her family in one night's raid on Norwich. One heard her husband was captured or killed in the Far East and one with a small child lost her pilot husband early in the war. There was no counselling we just helped each other through.

We were held up from crossing a parade ground at the R.A.F. station one day only to find that a brigade of W.A.A.F. had come under fire from a lone German fighter when they were drilling. We never found out how many were killed that day.

I finally moved to Nottinghamshire nearing the end of the war and worked with some P.O.W.s for a few days. The owner of the land I was to work on was ill so he sent his wife and me to a nearby P.O.W. camp at Tollerton to collect three prisoners. Arriving at the guard house we had to pass two Free Polish Army personnel then next two Free French Army and finally two British soldiers. I really wish I could put down in writing what they said but the air was blue! Behind them was this enormous compound full of German prisoners yelling, whistling and 'pretending' to climb over the wire. What happened next was hilarious, we rode our bikes back to the field we were working in and the prisoners were marched with a soldier, rifle at the ready, behind us. When we got to the field the soldier 'with the rifle' turned, he called, "will pick them up at five o-clock" and he was gone, leaving two young women with a sick farmer and three burly Germans, one with a look that said "Beware", he certainly wasn't for fraternising with. The other two were German students who spoke fairly good English and were easy to talk too but the odd one worked away from us all the time.

There are so many memories I could write but mainly I was lucky to have been in hostels where there was so much friendliness and companionship It was hard and the hostels were lacking in comfort but we did have regular working hours and weren't at the beck and call of farmers twenty four hours a day. Near the end I had severe back problems and was eventually invalided out. I spent seven months cased in plaster and four decades in a steel ribbed support. I got no compensation or pension. On my eightieth birthday in 2003, the guest of honour was my friend Joyce, we had met on that first day, I was her bridesmaid in June 1944 and then we lost touch with each other for almost sixty years, but that's another story.

NOTE. A little extra information regarding Marion's stay in Nottingham has emerged. Marion was stationed at Coddington, near Newark and the hostel there had a German woman warden who was required to report to the police each day. One weekend when the girls had all gone home there was a break in at the hostel. The Warden got her son, also a German to come and the police soon realised that the incident was planned and after a few weeks the son was removed.

Marion also served at Bunny hostel for a short time and her last job in Nottinghamshire was at Kirby-in-Ashfield working on the sugar beet with the farmer. This farmer praised her for working so well (something that was lacking before) and eventually his report on her back problem secured her release for the Land Army.

Miriam Cobley nee Hopper.   Holton Le Clay, Grimsby
I have received quite a good amount of information and pictures from Miriam and it is clear that at some stage recently she has attended a meeting and given a talk on her experiences in the Land Army. Miriam sent me a copy of that talk which is reproduced in full.

After my parents refused their consent for me to join the ATS, I came up with the idea of the Land Army. No more problems, they thought I would be safe from any undesirable people in that. Mother insisted she went with me to the Enrolment Office (parents did that in my days). In there was another girl a little older than me (no mother) and my mother immediately asked the Enrolment Officer if we could go together. Now we had never met this girl, we knew nothing about her or her background but of course, if she was going in the Land Army she must be suitable.

The first posting for 2 girls was for general farm work (we asked for horticulture), it was close to my home (my parents were pleased, so was Minnie) I had hoped to go further afield. So on the 4th of April 1942 we duly arrived at Glebe Farm, West Halton nr. Scunthorpe, in Minnie's previous employer's car, (my first ride in a car!). He gave us a gramophone and some dance records, which enabled Minnie to teach me to dance. I had never been allowed to go to dance halls.

Arriving after the farm labourers were already at work, we were given the job of beating 2 carpets that were hanging on the line, no more domestic jobs except our own room. Minnie and I shared a double bed with a straw mattress which was hard but seemed to alleviate any aches and pains we suffered with. We spent most evenings in our own room; there were no activities in the village, only a pub which we never visited. Our main occupation in the evenings was dancing as I've said, sewing, darning our woollen socks and writing letters (Wilton was in the Middle

East by now), washing our clothes, ourselves and our hair. Mine was short and permed no trouble. We were often taken for twins or at least sisters. We did get on very well and became great friends.

Mr Brown was looked after by his two spinster sisters who cooked our meals and on Mondays made apple turnovers for the week. By Friday they were mouldy, but the birds and mice ate them, we didn't. Our lunch pack up was mainly cheese because we got extra rations of that.

I was given the biggest of 8 horses in the stables, a Shire horse called Captain, we loved each other on sight, I had had nothing to do with horses or the land before and I took to it like a duck to water. When one of the men picked up a stick and for what reason I can't remember threatened to hit Captain, I grabbed the stick and told him in a language he understood what I would do with it if he ever hit one of the horses again. However, even I had to be careful, one day when I walked behind Captain and without thinking touched him on the rump before I spoke, he kicked me on the shin but thankfully only bruised it, very painful but I never did it again. Another horse in the next stall to Captain, a small Arab, bit me on the chest as I turned away from talking to Captain. I had two rows of teeth marks down my chest, glad she hit centre!

Springtime was the nicest because that was when Captain and I did the harrowing and rolling ready for seeding, which was done by Mr Kershaw, the oldest farmhand and our mentor whilst we were at the farm. Before I could do this I had to learn how to put Captain's collar on and get him to put his head down so that I could reach him, he was very good. I had to learn to back him between the shafts because if his heels touched the wood he would kick out and could smash the wagon etc. Another spring job was broadcasting fertilizer, not a nice one! A hopper was strapped to your front, as you walked you took a handful of fertilizer and threw it first one side and then the other, alright on a still day!

The most back breaking spring job was planting potatoes. We were helped by the women from the village that had been doing it for years and we were expected to keep up

The men would cut and lay the hay, then Captain and I would use the hay rake to turn it several times till it dried. Then we had to hand rake it and pile it onto the dray which carried it to the stack yard, where we built a stack and were taught how to thatch the stack with straw for weather proofing. On one occasion I jumped down from the dray onto a mound of hay which slid under my feet. I fell backwards and hit my head on the wheel hub. I got up laughing saying it's a good job my heads wooden too.

Beetroot for Breakfast!

Mr Kershaw said I don't think it is. I was wearing a pale green turban and when I took it off it was red! I went back to the farm to report the accident to Mr Brown and he said you had best get on your bike and go up to see the doctor at Winterton, up hill all the way. He then remembered the local nurse was in the village at a neighbouring farm and thought that if I went there she would be able to patch me up, which I did, I could walk there.. When the nurse saw the wound she knew it needed stitching so I told her what Mr Brown had said. The farmer rang Mr Brown and said in a few choice words that he was to get his car out and take me up to the doctors himself, which he did. I had 4 stitches and no headache; I told you it was wooden!

In the summer we dug drains and laid pipes, weeding and thinning root crops, thistle cutting, cereal weeding etc. During the summer we had several Irishmen come to the farm, they stayed in an old railway carriage and looked after themselves. Their job was to pick up potatoes after the spinner and transport them to the cart, where I was sitting. I would then take them to the pie at the edge of the field which was then covered with straw and earth.

Autumn time and our first job of the harvest was hand scything a path for the horses and reaper so that they could access the corn without damage. The job of cutting the corn was dome by the men, we had to pick up the sheaves and put them together in stooks of 8 to allow the wind to dry them out before they could be stacked. Wheat was the heaviest, oats were the lightest and barley the dirtiest and the most uncomfortable because the awns stuck to your skin, scratched you and got under your clothes. When the corn was dry we had to throw the sheaves up to a person on the wagon, tiring (Harvest time meant long hours often till dark) The wagon would then go to the stack yard where the sheaves were built into stacks and then thatched., though some stacks were made in the field where they stayed until spring.

Winter – spread muck (OK manure) after cleaning out the cattle sheds and stables first. A good job for winter, it kept you warm. Chopping mangle wurzles for cattle food after lifting them - usually on a cold and frosty morning. Lifting sugar beet and piling it on the side of the road for the lorries to pick up and take to the Brigg sugar beet factory.

Another winter job was riddling the potatoes. The potatoes were scooped out of the pie and thrown on the riddle which shook some of the dirt off and discarded the small ones which would get fed to the pigs, 2 or 3 people stood each side of the machine picking off any bad ones. The good ones went into bags which were loaded onto a dray and taken to the branch line and sent off to Scunthorpe.

I cut hedges with a hedging knife, very satisfying to see a nice clean hedge and a straight top. We used sickles to clean out weeds etc. and cleared the ditches (pity they don't do more of this now). I was taught how to sharpen my scythe and sickle and clean all the tools I used and oil them before putting them away.

Soon the threshing machine would come chugging into the yard and a mountain of coal would be delivered. This was a job I didn't like. When working on the stack which had been standing for months, mice were everywhere. It seemed that every sheaf was home to a family of them. I know I had string tied below my knees so they couldn't get up my trousers, but I didn't like it, I never got used to it. However, I didn't show my fear because I knew the men would probably throw some at me. One of them did chase Minnie round and round the stack yard with a rat until she was hysterical (no farmer around when you wanted him). It was at threshing time when Minnie was killed. The horse came back into the yard fully loaded but no Minnie. She was found injured in the road. Somehow the wagon had gone over her right shoulder, her rib punctured her lung but it was the shock that killed her. I was on the machine feeding sheaves into it when this happened. I remember we carried on, there was nothing we could do and she died that night.

Mr Brown's sisters decided to leave soon after, so that meant I had to be re-housed. I was billeted with the Foreman but not for long, his wife didn't like it and she ruled the roost.

Mt next billet was with Mr and Mrs Burgess in Alkborough (2 miles away). OK but when I got home at night I had to get undressed and washed in the outhouse before I was allowed in the house. While living here I joined the Women's Institute and met Ethel Thornton I also joined Keep Fit and the Glee Club.

I was alone on the farm for the next year and during this year I did all the same jobs as the men. I remember standing one leg each side of a sheaf half way up the roof of a stack, catching the sheaves with a 2 tyne pitchfork as the men threw them up to me and helping them on their way up to Mr Kershaw for him to lay in place.. One at a time was fine but then the men thought it would be fun to see if I could catch 2 at a time. Not wanting to appear a weakling I continued to catch them (that's where I went wrong). The men then tried 3, now my temper was getting up so I dropped them, which meant they had to throw them up again. I told them to stop it or I would throw my fork down instead of dropping the sheaves. They just laughed (up to now I had never shown my temper so they were quite sure I wouldn't do it). The next lot of sheaves came up, I ignored them and threw my fork at them and caught one of them on the thigh. Game over.

In 1944, my sister Barbara came of age to do war work. My mother said she was too delicate to do factory work or nursing and of course, no ATS. The only way she could join the WLA at that time was if I asked my farmer if she could join me as he was supposed to have 2 land girls. Fortunately he said yes but there was no room for her at the Burgess's as I was already sleeping with their young daughter in a double bed. Mrs Ethel Thornton (who had 2 sons away in the Army) offered us accommodation sharing a bed, we were used to that at home. She was lovely and I kept in touch with her until she died. Her husband Joe worked as a butcher in Scunthorpe so we never went hungry. Ethel kept chickens at the bottom of the garden, so it was cooked breakfast every morning, a good pack up and a good hot meal every night. Heaven after the other billets.

Christmas 1944 – Wilton arrived home and we were married on 1st January, a New Year, a new life. I joined him down at Okehampton but I was living with Wilton and working with a gang of girls who lived in a hostel so never got to know them. The gang were sent to which ever farmer needed labour, they were monotonous jobs, and the only highlight of that time was when we were sent to pick potatoes. Now, as I have told you I never did that on my farm. We duly arrived in our truck and the first thing the farmer said was I want one of you girls to lead the horse and cart' Dead silence and horrified looks all round. So I piped up and said, "OK I'll do it", relief all round. I still never picked a potato, I had the cushiest job of all.

Wilton was having so much free time that I eventually left the Land Army and helped a local nurseryman with the understanding that if Wilton was free I didn't go to work. After 4 years apart, this time in Devon gave us time to get to know each other.

We celebrated the end of the war dancing to the Floral Dance.

WOMEN'S LAND ARMY (ENGLAND AND WALES).
RELEASE CERTIFICATE.

The Women's Land Army for England and Wales acknowledges with appreciation the services given by

Mrs. Cobley

who has been an enrolled member for the period from

4. 5. 1942 to 7. 7. 1945

and has this day been granted a willing release.

Date 7. 7. 45.

E. M. Raglin

COUNTY SECRETARY. WOMEN'S LAND ARMY (DEVON)

Miriam Cobley at home 2009

Beetroot for Breakfast!

Miriam Cobley nee Hopper

Miriam Cobley nee Hopper at home (2009)

152

Claire Leith nee Oats.   Truro, Cornwall.

I have received a couple of letters and a commentary from Claire Leith who resides in Cornwall so I will include her story with extracts from each.

Somewhere there is a number, I mean mine as a member of the Women's Land Army and I am glad still to have my old badge but do not look for laurels or praise. What we all did was try to help our country in her great need and did our duty.

I was born at our home in Porthledden, Cape Cornwall in St. Just-in –Penwith in February 1922. I left school in 1939 in Sussex and my aunt came on holiday from Slinfold. When she returned I went with her and immediately joined up in Horsham and did my training at Slinfold Farm.

In hindsight I felt that I didn't shine at my duties so, no farm and shipped off to the woods. I seemed to have difficulty in getting milk out of cows and let the turkey poults out in the rain and then got entangled by the strings of my apron in the bottle washing machine... So, by and by I found myself on a train platform in Lincoln plus others, bound for Bourne in Lincolnshire. I was billeted with Mr and Mrs Kew, in the little main street and here I was truly blessed in these two lovely people at once, so kind and helpful and we remained friends for life. Babs, my fellow land girl had been a mannequin in London but did not stay very long.

We all somehow arrived at the HUT in Bourne Forest and at some moment all handed a heavy black, but serviceable bike and on that we not only went to and fro 5 days a week to work but had the inestimable use of over our marvellous free weekends. (I realised how free we were when I later landed upon a dairy farm and we milked at FIVE A.M.)

There were some 20 girls in our Gang and we all soon knew each other, mostly from London way or far up in the North Durham way, but, as at school we all had our 'chums' but I do not remember us mixing in our billets. I do remember once lending a Durham lass money to go home where some tragedy had struck and could only do so as my honoured parents had given me £10 as a 'nest egg' to be used only in case of emergency.

In the woods we were in the charge of an elderly woodsman,

Mr Tupman and a younger one (I think exempt from 'Call-up' for health reasons). We were a merry crowd and we had many tasks from weeding

153

tiny saplings to cutting down biggish trees and from sawing up logs to pruning or layering various trees or bushes like hazels.

As I said, the bikes were a tremendous asset and I had happy times learning the layout near at hand and now, all these years on, am remembering the cuckoos. I've never often seen or heard so many announcing Spring after the very cold snow drifty Winter and not often experienced in Cornwall. These staunch horses (the bikes) took us far and wide, most frequently to Grantham where we could luxuriate in a bath at the free Public Baths (We were scrubbed okay at the Kews every Friday or Saturday pm and the copper kept bubbling and the hot fire to dry by – heavenly!) Afterwards, Mr Kew with his handy maps and helpful instruction followed by, to me - a <u>new</u> meal-time about 9pm, more or less left-overs from high tea, when we came in from the woods.

The Kews had a daughter away nursing and a son Harold in the R.A.F., who came home off and on. I, of course, was an R.A.F. girl with my brother a Flight Commander and myself with a favourite Pilot (boy friend) Spitfires and Grantham, home to the Bomber aerodromes beside the town. We well knew the Lancaster's drone and sometimes the odd one waggled his wings over the wood and of course we all downed tools and waved and cheered madly.

Grantham also held snug pubs, not that we were boozers, only camaraderie, precious in those days. Once or twice when we were 'in funds' we trained to Nottingham and a good live show at the Playhouse... But the bikes took us to further places, to Folkingham, to Sleaford and to Lincoln City itself once or twice... Here I was witness at a wedding of a close friend Betty from Streat when she married Skid Haines, a Canadian fighter pilot and was soon to be posted to Tunis.

It was this Betty and self who were chosen to go collecting acorns. We were instructed to fill an outsize bag that day, to be collected, both the sack and ourselves about 4pm. The site was on a fairly busy road and beneath some great oaks. We collected like wizards and no stop for croust (Cornish for elevenses) and lo, the sack full, we tied it up and hey presto, soon a lift to Grantham and some light refreshment.

I was again told I would be sent to Colsterworth for a month or two and some others from Bourne wood too. One was Molly, a big strapping girl from London who wielded a 7lb axe a treat! We were lodged in a farmhouse and there I think I could take you but the name of the farmer and the farmhouse, I forget. I hold clearly in my memory the little able wife and her front parlour where I was closeted when getting over a bad cold... We all used to eat in the big kitchen and stay in the warm until bedtime and I used to tell them stories – I've never done it since but here it seemed quite natural.

I seem to eat the pages up and there is still plenty more but I'll try to wind up. Remembering tho' the little ACK- ACK battery on a little knoll not far out of Rippingale so we had soldiery as well to enjoy and called on them if not 'on watch' at some parts over the weekend.

Some of us left to go to farm jobs, Betty being one. After 6 months and when we were due to have some leave I got a bad mark. I simply took time off to hitch to Scotland in search of my R.A.F. pilot and when I returned the faithful KEWS had been beset by queries from the Landgirl Representative. Anyhow as far as I was concerned I said (from Cornwall) I would not work anywhere else but Lincolnshire and they relented and I next landed up at Boothby Pagnell, not far from Spitalgate and Grantham and the Boys in Blue. I had a billet 2 miles out but the little family suffered a sad loss in the illness and death of their dear little 3 year old son. So it was arranged that I should have my billet in Boothby Hall, the garden of which I use to work in, under the old gardener. Mr Right (or Wright). I was also happily loaned out to a big farm (not far from Happy Valley) during the hay and corn harvest. Much gardening details at the Hall etc. but by now, if you are not asleep you cannot be far off that pleasant peace! So, dear John Ward, pick what you like and use your weaving skills and the best of good wishes.

I loved my time in the Land Army with some reservations!!

Claire Leith nee Oats
with Risky - 1941

'The Four Stooges'
Lyn, Betty, Claire and Mollie.

*Claire Leith nee Oats
now lives in Cornwall*

Boothby Hall

I have received a short letter from a Mr J Matthews of Morton, near Gainsborough, Lincolnshire regarding a former member of the Women's Land Army Unfortunately Mr Matthews tells me nothing of the life of Miss **Elizabeth Bostock** whilst she served with the Land Army from 29th July 1941 until 3rd September 1949

Miss Bostock was born in Basford, Nottingham and bought up in Ilkeston, Derbyshire. It is interesting to note that she became the Mayor of Ilkeston for 1952 to 1953 and received the Queen's Coronation Medal.

LINDSEY WOMEN'S LAND ARMY

Lincoln

W.L.A. Office,
6 Lindum Road,
Lincoln.

Dear *Miss Bostock*.

I am happy to congratulate you on your continued good service in the Women's Land Army, resulting in the award of a further Good Service Badge. Your work is very much appreciated by all concerned.

Yours sincerely,

[signature]

County Secretary

Mr W R Hobbs   **Spalding, Lincolnshire**

Another short letter I have received came from a Mr W R Hobbs of Spalding, who wrote

"Dear Sir,

I was most interested in your request for Land Army Girls.

The enclosed snap was taken of girls who worked on a farm in South Kyme. I have two vivid memories of them one of which made me respect them greatly.

The first is of potato setting, which in those days was done entirely by hand. Anyone who does not know what it is like; it's like touching your toes for about five hours. Anyway, the first morning it nearly killed the girls after about two hours the Foreman said, "Take 10 minutes" The girls straightened up, some cried, some swore with language us country yokels had never heard before, they all said that they would be going home that night, the Land Army was over for them.

They all turned up next morning and were still there when I joined the Army.

The other thing I remember was the day that Gladys stuck the pitch fork tine through the middle of my hand.

They all came from South Yorkshire and had gone when I was demobbed.

Gladys married a local lad but died quite young. I never saw any of the other again. Sorry about the writing but at 84 my eyesight is not too good.

Yours faithfully

R. Hobbs.

Beetroot for Breakfast!

Betty Welton nee Rawlinson.   **Caistor, Lincolnshire**

"Just a line or two to say I was in the Land Army. I was nearly eighteen when I joined. I went from Wakefield, Westgate station on my own, to Aylesbury in Buckinghamshire, and joined hundreds of other girl there. We were sent for training at a hostel, then to Ingoldsby near Grantham and Little Ponton to a hostel. We did lots of different work and it was very hard. I had worked in a dress shop before joining up so it was a huge change for me.

While milking a cow in Buckinghamshire, a cow kicked out and sent me flying; I sprained my wrist and had to go home for a while.

My last post was at Branston, near Lincoln, where I was shepherdess and loved working with the sheep and lambs. I was at Branston when peace was declared and what a party we had.

I got married in Lincolnshire and I am still here, my age is 84. I have such good memories of the Land Army as it changed my life altogether
Yours sincerely
Betty Welton

PS. I enjoyed the service at Lincoln Cathedral a few months ago, for a big reunion it was very emotional, but it was an honour to meet up with everyone.

I met my first husband while at Branston and over the years we have had four children. We went to live at Swallow where he sadly died. I brought up my four children and finally met my second husband and had a happy life again.

While I was at Branston, a German fighter was overhead and machine gun fire went right down the roof of the terraced houses where we were lodging. Also we had to bath in the wash- house across the yard in a tin bath and my word it was cold in winter.
B.W.

The vast majority of ex land girls I have spoken with or received letters from are rightly proud of their service. Many, at times, thought the conditions hard but they prevailed and all came to enjoy the comradeship, freedom and the sense of duty which 'came with the job'.
I received only one letter where the above appears untrue

Mrs Elaine Price.   **Bilsthorpe, Nottinghamshire**

Dear John

I have a very small snippet about a Land Army girl. My Mother-in-Law; now deceased, related to me that she went, as a Land Army girl to Gringley-on-the-Hill, near Gainsborough. She hated it, cried a lot, she had to ride a rickety old bike to get around on the farm. She was eventually sent home as it was a hard life, she couldn't hack it. I think mucking the pigs out was instrumental as she would recognise the smell immediately, wherever she was.

Sorry but that's all she ever said. I don't know how old she was then, let's see – she died in 1994 at the age of 73 so she was born in 1921. She must have been 20-ish.

Yours sincerely

Elaine Price (Mrs)

Poems and Pieces.

Many girls in the Land Army used their spare time writing home and many composed poems to send to their families or simply as reminders of their experiences.

Poems and Pieces is a miscellany of poems, stories, interesting facts and figures (some gleaned from newspaper cuttings) which have emerged since I started writing. Acknowledgement is paid to the authors and other sources including copyright, where known and apologies offered for any omissions, accidental or unknown.

It was intended that when a girl joined the Land Army she would receive a copy of 'Land Girl' A Manual for Volunteers in the Women's Land Army, by W E Sherwell-Cooper. I have asked many ex. Land Girls if they received a copy of the booklet only to find two that remembers ever receiving a copy.

The following is an extract from the Handbook, Page 94:

'There are so many obvious things which get forgotten. The volunteer should always be punctual in her hours; she should not smoke about the place, especially in farm buildings; she should shut gates behind her; she should put tools back properly, so that the next person who wants them can find them; she should never leave a job half done just because she finds it difficult.

A farmer is not made in a month, and, after training, some girls are inclined to teach the farmer his business, often with unfortunate results. So if a volunteer has been taught a method different from the farmers, she should always ask his permission before making a change. Farmers have no time to bother with fussy volunteers. They expect girls who have offered to do the work to carry it out without complaint.

A volunteer who enrols to "see if she likes it" is a liability not an asset. However patriotic she may feel, she does not help her country by enrolling in the Land Army unless she is certain she can stay the course...

Hope.

Although this little poem was composed quite recently, the sentiments would have applied during the days of World War II.

Oh, listen to the bad news
That's all we ever hear,
You turn on the telly and it always brings a tear
With all those people starving
And a mugging every day,
There's only one thing we should do,
Get on our knees and pray.
Thank God for all the good things,
As we travel along life's way
And I am sure that very soon
We'll see a better day.

Marie Bannister - Branston, Lincolnshire.

There are cows at the bottom of our garden.

There are cows at the bottom of our garden,
I see them come each day
And they will eat most anything
Even what I throw away.

I have made a compost heap, that's meant for Spring manure
But they have eaten half of it
It really is a 'stewer'

There are cows at the bottom of our garden,
I can hear them on their way.
They always 'moo' at milking time
The best time of the day!

Beryl Firman
Billingborough, Lincolnshire

· · · · · · · ·

There was a young lady from Gloucester
Who was driving a cow when she loucester,
So she got a large bough
And followed that cough
And didn't she put it acrouster!

Anon.

· · · · · · · ·

164

A snippet sent in by Paul Adams of Lincoln, of a story told to him by **Audrey Stone,** sadly now deceased.

I was head of the Land Army Girls in this part of Lincolnshire. (believed to be Louth). One day I had to line the girls up for an inspection by Raine Spencer. She walked along, loftily passed my Girls, and finally reached me, when she said "Isn't it funny – my Mother says that one should never wear khaki, it reminds one of a potato!" and I turned to her and replied, "Well of course we have our Royal Blue uniforms, but we reserve them for very important visitors"

Note. Raine Spencer was the Dowager Countess Spencer, step mother of the late Princess Diana.

· · · · · · · ·

Land Girls at Work.
We met on the Midland Station,
In Nineteen Forty Two.
All were young and carefree,
We were off to pastures new.

Twenty Two young ladies
Were off to work the land.
All in spruce new uniforms
Complete with green armbands.

Down we went to Beaulieu,
To the house of Lady Dent.
You see, for her war effort
This lovely house she'd lent.

We toiled in wet cold winters
And summer's searing heat.
Often we had backache,
Or tender, swollen feet.

But we made the best of it
In spite of the poor grub
And had a bit of fun at night,
Down at the local pub.

Many years have passed along
Since those wartime years.
We tend to forget the problems,
Hard work, poor pay and fears.

We remember all the good things,
The laughter and the fun.
Village 'hops' and dancing
When the long hard day was done.

Now in Nineteen Eighty Nine
A few of us have lunch.
We remember, laugh and talk
While we sit and munch.

Sadly our numbers have dwindled,
But we have some memories to treasure.
So when we meet at the 'Royal'
We sit and talk at leisure.

Edna Keena
Nottingham

(Taken from 'Land Army Days. Cinderellas of the Soil' by Knighton
Joyce.)

. . . .

166

Another little offering from **Marie Bannister** of Branston.

A Land Army Prayer.

Oh Heavenly Father, if it's in thy power
Send us down a heavy shower.
If you send it, send it quick
So that we don't have to 'pick'

Picking potatoes pick to win the War,
Whenever you think you've picked enough
Get down and pick some more!

· · · · · · · ·

To All Land Girls.

I saw a land girl working
Alone in an open field.
Her, hard, once elegant hands
A stalwart hoe did yield.
Her back was bent as she slew the weeds
That spoiled the potatoes' growth;
She never wilted, she never paused,
She had taken her silent oath.

At last the day was nearly done,
The sun was sinking low;
She gathered up her jacket
Then slowly cleaned her hoe.
She passed the chair where I sat
(I'm feeble in body and sight).
She smiled at me as she said,
"Been hot today, Goodnight"

We hear the valiant deeds of our men in "furrin parts"
Deeds which bring the tears to our eyes,
a glow of pride to our hearts-
But when the war is over and peace at last restored,
I shall always remember the Land Girl,
who made her hoe her sword.
Anon - From an admirer of their work.

167

Lord Woolton was the Minister of Food and he devised
a new version of a nursery rhyme.

Ministry of Food Advertisement.

Because of the pail, the scraps were saved,
Because of the scraps, the pigs were saved,
Because of the pigs, the rations were saved,
Because of the rations, the ships were saved,
Because of the ships, the island was saved,
Because of the island, the Empire was saved,
And all because of the housewife's pail.

. . . .

The Boots Company, Nottingham. – Hill Farm.

In the past The Boots Company used to publish an in-house magazine
entitled 'The Mixture' and in the October 1942 issue it featured an article
on Hill Farm, Thurgarton, Nottinghamshire.

The Boots Company acquired Hill Farm in 1941 with a view to
establishing a Veterinary Research Station. The Company had already
the Lenton Experimental Grounds where approximately 200 retail staff
members spent a few days during a Horticultural Course in 1941.

The author of the article J P Byron gave an overview of the situation of
the farm and the intentions to re-structure the buildings for purpose. The
farm was of 300 acres (125 acres grassland and 175 acres of arable land)
situated some 12 miles from Nottingham. Almost every field had a direct
entry from the road and water was laid on every pasture. Local history
tells us that the surrounding area and probably Hill Farm too was farmed
by the Monks of Thurgarton Priory (their water mill was sited at nearby
Fiskerton).

The primary object of Hill Farm was developing a research centre
for the investigation of animal pests and diseases and their control and
treatment.

Considerable structural alterations were required to make the farm fit
for purpose and this was achieved under the guidance and management
of Mr S Williams MSc. NDA, an experienced man in connection with
agricultural problems in many countries. Mr William's staff included
two Land Girls billeted at the farm, who, between them did most of the
milking which began at 6am and carried out by hand before milking

machines were eventually installed.

The dairy herd consisted of pedigree Ayrshire's, 20 of which were in-milk at the time. A number of calves were born at the farm. In addition to the Ayrshires there was a bunch of Herefords used for fattening and they produced manure for bountiful crops. There were also 80 sheep and a number of pigs plus a few poultry so the girls really had their work cut out for them.

Difficulty was experienced in obtaining suitable farming implements. The Unit boasted a Fordson tractor on rubber tyres and shortly afterwards a Caterpiller D2. The farm also had four Shire mares and a black cob – horse, not easy to buy in those days. The farm was successful and certainly enhanced its prestige in the farming world giving the farmer confidence in Boots products.

In 1935 Boots launched its No.7 beauty products so it wasn't a surprise to find a Land Girl advertising their products.

I have spoken with ex. Land girls who had actually worked at Hill Farm and other farms in the area when required.

Shown in this photograph are staff members from Boots, Cheltenham Spa Branch helping out in the fields at Hill Farm. In the foreground are Miss D Fennall, Miss J Arnold and Miss D Bond. Nothing more is known of these three ladies or the two Land Girls employed at Hill Farm.
(Photograph courtesy of The Boots Co. (Archives)

number seven

beauty preparations by Boots

CLEANSING CREAM 1..., 4..., LEMON CREAM 3...
COMPLEXION MILK 1..., SKIN TONIC 2.4, 4.6, 4.6
ASTRINGENT LOTION 2.6, SKIN FOOD 2.6, 3.6
MUSCLE OIL 2.6, HAND LOTION 2.6, FOUNDATION
CREAM 1..., FOUNDATION LOTION 2.6, FACE
CLEANSING TISSUES 2..., FACE POWDER IN
NINE SHADES 1..., BEAUTY BOXES 10.6, 21...,
15..., AND, OF COURSE, COSMETICS, LIPSTICK,
ROUGE, ROUGE CREAM, EYE SHADOW AND
EYELASH COSMETIQUE, ALL IN MANY SHADES

The scene has changed from Mayfair to the muddy fields of the shires. The smart frock has given place to the breeches and leggings of the Land Army. Yet, despite rough work and exposure to all weathers, her loveliness remains unmarred. For care of beauty is neither costly nor troublesome with Number Seven preparations. Made perfect by more than fifty years of Boots' experience, they are as effective in the rustic billet as they were in the well-appointed boudoir.

Fresh fields for Beauty . . .

Fresh fields for Beauty.
A Land Girl advertises Boots No. 7 beauty preparations. (Courtesy The Boots Co.)

170

Tractors.

Many of the land girls had to drive a tractor in the course of their duties. The vast majority had never driven before and were introduced to the machines by the farmers. Tractor driving became an unavoidable part of the job especially for the members of the Timber Corps. Tractors played an increasing role in food production as more and more of the land was put to the plough after the Ministry of Agriculture and Fisheries offered a grant of £2 per acre..

At the outbreak of the war there were only three major tractor manufacturers in Britain, - Ford, David Brown and Marshalls, the Fordson Model N being the most popular. It was first produced in the Irish Republic and transferred to Dagenham in 1933 which then had a base price of £156. By the mid war years, the production was more than 100 tractors per days. Very few changes were made to the model but pneumatic tyres were an option in 1933. This model, the Fordson N was replaced in 1945 by the E27N. Between September 1939 and May 1945 (the war years) the factory in Dagenham produced 137,483 tractors.

David Brown had started to produce the Ferguson – Brown tractor in the mid 30's but had produced only 1,500 tractors by 1939, and by 1939 David Brown produced its own agricultural tractor... It quickly gained a reputation for reliability and economy but fewer than 1,000 were manufactured between 1939 and 1945. The industrial version was widely adopted by the RAF and the Fleet Air Arm as an aircraft tug.

Marshall's of Gainsborough started producing tractors in 1930 with a single cylinder diesel powered Lanz Bulldog. This was replaced in 1936 but never produced in large numbers. Again, fewer than 1,500 were manufactured over a 10 year period.

Other British based manufacturers also produced tractors during the war, albeit in small numbers. British tractor production for the war years was 158,000 and by the end of the war more than 200,000 tractors were in use.

As in the war at sea, help came from the USA under the 1941 Lend-Lease arrangement and the farming industry was boosted by a supply of American built tractors, the majority being of the Ford 2N and 9N type. 10,000 were shipped to Britain along with others and British farmers had become acquainted with the John Deere, Case I.H. and Massey-Harris.

Some 6.5 million acres of grassland was ploughed up and put to food production during the war making a total of 19 million acres devoted to the production of food. Success!

Beetroot for Breakfast!

(Facts and figures by kind permission of 'Tractor and Faming' magazine, October 2009 edition)

· · · · · · · ·

From a Land Army Girl to her Mother - 1940

Dear Mam,
You won't believe what I have done,
Since I joined the Women's Land Army,
Six months away from Camden Town,
My boyfriend thinks I'm barmy.

I've tried my hand at milking,
Scared, thought it was a bull,
The nights are cold and very short,
My days are long and full.

Learned tractor driving, feeding pigs,
All from the break of day.
Hands, red and rough from picking spuds,
That Adolf's going to pay!

Done, ploughing, reaping, seeding,
Even apple picking.
Last night I ran near half a mile
To catch a bleeding chicken.

They say it's helping all our lads,
That's serving overseas,
Right now I need a cup of char,
Feet up and Player's Please.

They calls it Bomber County,
In famous Lincolnshire
My heart stops when the planes fly out.
Makes me proud that I work here.

Anon.

(Reproduced by kind permission of Heritage Lincolnshire from
'Lincolnshire Women at War')

If you want to go to Heaven when you die,
Wear a pair of Khaki breeches and a tie.
Wear an old felt bonnet, with WLA on it
If you want to go to Heaven when you die.
Quoted by Shirley Joseph.

· · · · · · · ·

Marie Bannister nee DeWael was employed at various farms while she was billeted at Mere Hostel near Branston. On one of the farms was a labourer named Maurice White, hence the following:

Up and down the field we go
Maurice at the wheel.
You'd be surprised the things he does
He often made us squeal!
We asked him, "Can we have a fag
Or else a cup of tea?"
He'd just ignore the things we say,
No matter how we plead
But on the whole he's not too bad,
He has his job to do,
So let's forget about the fags
And get some gum to chew.

· · · · · · · ·

Mention has already been made about the Handbook which each volunteer was supposed to have received, although very few ever did. One lady from Scunthorpe saw the amusing side of some of the directives given.

Handbook - Page 25. **How to Join**.
Resignations and Dismissals.
It is possible for a volunteer to resign for urgent private reasons or reasons of health. Volunteers, however, are reminded that

money has been spent on them to make them specialists for a vital job, so they should never resign unless *absolutely* necessary: "*You* are feeding the nation; if you drop out someone may starve."

Comment - Patriotic? Talk about the guilt trip!

· · · · · · · ·

My War Effort.

In forty-one fate brought us here
To work and play and worry,
We left behind our families dear
For England's name to carry.
We did not know what lay in store,
But knew we'd do our best,
With all our strength and evermore,
For each there'd be no rest.
From early morn 'til late at night,
In sun and rain, in wind and snow,
Our thresher worked with all its might.
And we four girls just let it go.
Here comes Jerry, let's dive for the ditch,
Low over the hedges he drops his load,
Narrowly missing our threshing pitch,
Leaving its mark right up the road.
But five minutes later we're back with the seed,
There's work to be done, a war to be won.
An army of men we need to feed,
A young girl's father, a mother's son
Have given their all for peace to be won.
Memories are precious, that no one can steal,
As we sit and ponder and think of the past.
For now peace has come, we pray God it will last.

Marion Andrews
(from 'War time Women' - Michael Bentinck 1998)

· · · · · · · ·

Handbook Page 65. **Employment**. Milk-round

A certain number of volunteers are employed by producer- retailers on milk rounds. The work consists of looking after horses, going out early on dark mornings, selling the milk, keeping the books, collecting the bottles and cheering up the housewives!

In addition there is a certain amount of work to be done in the dairy or with the cows themselves.

Comment. "cheering up the housewives", lovely comment was there time to spare? (60 hour week!)

·········

The Land Army Song.

Back to the Land, we must all lend a hand,
To the farms and the fields we must go.
There's a job to be done,
Though we can't fire a gun
We can still do our bit with a hoe.

Back to the Land, with its clay and its sand,
Its gravel and granite and grit.
You grow barley and wheat
And potatoes to eat
To make sure that the Nation keeps fit.

We will tell you once more
You can help win the war
If you come with us- back to the Land.

Quoted by W E Shewell-Cooper
(author of the Handbook)

·········

Margaret Bell nee Short of Branston, Lincolnshire, has written a couple of short stories for the Lincolnshire Poacher' magazine and with the author's permission and that of the magazine, the stories are reproduced.

Working With Knives.

My first encounter with knives was when I was a child about ten years old. Myself and my brother were laying the table for dinner. We both wanted the old square handled knife.

I was holding the blade, and he had hold of the handle.

We both held tight and pulled!

My index finger was cut into the bone. I resisted my mother's wish to see what was done and I had my finger bandaged, still bent under. Luckily the finger healed well.

At the age of eighteen I joined the Women's Land Army. On the farm, my first job was to cut down yellow ragwort, a tall weed that is poisonous to horses.

Myself and two other WLA girls were each given a long handled knife, and sent into a large grass field to cut down the ragwort, chopping as low as we could to the roots. Picture: three young girls swinging long blades. We soon got the knack, but it was a big field and a long day.

We were taught to use the fearsome stack knife, which was always left pushed into the stack where last used. We used to climb up a ladder to where a square had been cut out, and then had to stand, and with the huge blade, cut deeply down into the straw and along two sides then push the heavy cutting knife safely into the stack side ready for next time.

The hay fork was then plunged into the square of straw to carry it down the ladder.

The long handled hoes were for weeding the potatoes or sugar beet, and had to be sharp to do their job well.

We were taught how to use a file or a carborundum stone. It was hard work to get a good edge, and easy to cut a finger. Trimming knives were used to trim the leaves from the heavy mangolds. After taking them from the graves in the spring they had grown new leaves and they were a very pretty, pink, green and yellow. They were chopped in a machine and mixed with chaff for food for the cattle.

Then we used the sugar beet knife. A handy tool combining a hook to pick up the beet, heavy with leaves, and put it in the other hand then cut the top off with a quick movement and throw the beet onto a heap. One can get to work very quickly but it is easy to make a slip and cuts were frequent.

We used heavy trimming hooks to trim out the brush wood before bungling the twigs for kindling.

We were also taught how to use a scythe, but never to sharpen one. There was no Health and Safety in those days!

Always in my smock pocket was my pocket knife, about four inches long with white sides (less likely to get lost if dropped) this was kept sharp to cut the binder bands and to peel apples, turnip or cheese at lunch time.

I still have a few scars.

········

The following article appeared in The Dukeries Advertiser on 6th July 1984

Memories of the Women's Land Army.
by Sarah Jenkin-Jones.

Joining the Women's Land Army in the second World War was, for three town girls, like taking a jump into the deep end.

They took the place of men working on farms around Newark and Collingham, married farmers they had worked for, and have stayed in the area since.

Mrs Lillian Woolfitt now lives in Winthorpe with the farmer she married 40 years ago (1944) – Ted Woolfitt. She joined the Land Army in 1941 when she was 19 and was the first bride in the hostel.

Mrs Cynthia Shaw joined in 1942 when she was 20. She married Collingham farmer Frank Swift soon after leaving the Land Army in 1946. Mrs Shaw moved from Nottingham where she had been working in Griffin and Spalding (now Debenhams).

"I joined because I didn't want to work in the ammunition factory, we all had to do out bit for the war effort" she said.

Mrs Joan Baston moved to Collingham in 1943 when she was 18. She married agricultural contractor Mr Laurence Baston soon after leaving the hostel in 1950. *"I tried for the WAAF but was not tall enough so I decided to join the Land Army"* she said.

Mrs Baston had previously worked at Boots in the research dept. in Nottingham.

All three had no idea what was in store for them.

"My first reaction was to cry, I cried all day whilst doing my first job, picking carrots" said Mrs Baston.

Said Mrs Woolfitt, *"It was the quiet that struck me at first, I was used to the noise of town"*

Mrs Shaw was an only child and it was a new experience to live with 50 other girls in a hostel. *"I was very shy but the Land Army really brought me out of myself"* she said. *"At first many farmers did not like the idea of girls working on farms. Once you were accepted and proved your mettle, you were alright"*

Mrs Woolfitt said, *"My hardest job was milking a cow, before I went to Collingham I didn't even know what a cow was"*!

Some of the girls learnt to plough. The machinery was fuelled by steam and most jobs were done by hand or with the help of horses.

The women agreed that the worst job was picking potatoes and carrots. They had to gather the vegetables, *"stooping near the ground – a sure cause of backache"*

The girls started work at 7.30 am, dressed in dungarees, shirts, jumpers and overcoats. Most of them had to walk to the farms before they learnt how to ride bicycles. Mrs Baston had more trouble than most mastering this skill, her main problem was in turning corners.

"The hostel in Woodhall Road, Collingham, was like a cowshed with double bunks flanking the concrete floored rooms" said Mrs Baston. *"There was a chest of drawers and a wardrobe between two; three baths, two showers and several basins"*

"We were allowed only 4 inches of water in a bath" said Mrs Shaw.

It was not all work. *"We worked hard and played hard"* said Mrs Baston. Girlish pranks were rife and Mrs Baston recounted a time they tied a girl to a chair and left her outside in the snow because she insisted that she loved the snow.

Said Mrs Shaw, *"One of the reasons we all got on so well was that, in wartime you did not know whether you would be there the next day"*

The area was full of RAF camps; there was no shortage of dances to attend.

Mrs Baston said, *"My best-ever dance was after we'd been to a pub in Eagle. We had picked primroses in the woods and put them in our hair. The RAF lads dropped their WAAF girls and took us to the dance instead"*

179

Beetroot for Breakfast!

Going to the pictures in Newark meant a long walk home after missing the last train.

"Looking back on it all I do not know how we stuck it, especially in winter" said Mrs Shaw.

Mrs Woolfitt said, *"They were great days and it is 40 years on, ten of us still meet once a month and find things to talk about"*

*Collingham Hostel, Woodhall Road, Collingham
as it is today. (2009)*

Lest We Forget.

Our soldiers and sailors and airmen bold,
We're proud that you fought, our country to hold.
Those who fought and did return,
You've kindled a flame in our hearts to burn.
We'll think of you in these days of Peace.

But those who were lost in the fiery stream,
True affection reigns in out hearts supreme.
Slumber peacefully in your hero's grave
You fought very bravely, our Empire to save.

And we will remember in days to come,
Tis through fellows like you, we still have a home.
Though we cannot quite see a better World yet
May we never forget, may we never forget.

Beryl Firman nee Bestwick.
Billingborough, Lincolnshire

Another snippet from the Handbook.
No comment is made on this contribution
as I am sure the reader will see
the funnier side of some of the
suggestions offered in the extract.

Making the Most of the Country.
The town girl does not often find it easy to live in the country. She naturally misses all the amenities that she is used to. She cannot pop into the local cinema when she feels inclined. She cannot even go round to the local fish and chip shop or to a snack bar if she wants a quick meal in the evening. She is not able to stroll down the High Street and have a look at the shops and see the latest fashions, and there are not, of course, the number of men about to go to dances with at the local Palais de Dance.

Some town people are apt to look upon all country folk as country bumpkins. They have an idea that it is only the town folk who know anything, and because people in the country are not so slick, or not so well dressed, or perhaps are not up to the latest fashion, they are apt to be labelled old-fashioned and rather a back number.

Actually, country folk usually know far more than those who are bred and born in towns and cities. They may not know all the names of the film stars and pictures in which they have appeared, but they do know the names of the birds and their habits. They are able to tell whether it is going to be wet or fine the next day. They know which herbs are useful and all about the ways of wild animals. They have a different kind of knowledge that is all.

The Land Army volunteer, therefore, who is going to work on a farm and live in a village must be prepared to see 'the other fellow's' point of view. She will never be a success if she goes into her new surroundings determined to show them a thing or two. She will only be stared at if she wears the latest Bond Street creation at the local social or 'hop.' She will be considered rude if she is continually saying, "Fancy you not knowing that", or is constantly boasting of her doings in the town.

It does need a little effort at first to fit in with new surroundings. It is always necessary to consider the farmer and his family; to consider the billeter, and remember to help in the little things, and to lend a hand sometimes without being asked.

There are many obvious things which get forgotten. The volunteer should always be punctual in her hours; she should not smoke about the place, especially in farm buildings; she should shut gates behind her; she should put tools back properly, so that the next person who wants them can find them; she should never leave a job half done just because she finds it difficult.

Make-up – Town girls on the whole use far more make-up than country girls. The Women's Land Army volunteer should therefore be prepared to 'tone down' her lips, complexions and nails considerably.

A certain amount of make-up may be used at parties and local village dances, but long nails are quite unsuited for work on the farm, especially when covered in bright crimson nail varnish.

The volunteer will soon find that, as the other girls from the village do not use make-up, she will prefer not to use it herself, so as not to look conspicuous. She will find too, that she will get such a healthy colour to her cheeks that rouging will not be necessary.

No Comment!

Beetroot for Breakfast!

I had made arrangements to visit **Ivy Woodliffe** at her home at Norwell Woodhouse, Nottinghamshire prior to Christmas 2009 but unfortunately she became ill and passed away shortly afterwards. I did however visit her son in law at Southwell but he was not able to tell me much about Ivy. She still lived on a farm prior to her passing and, as a land girl working at Tuxford during the war she appears to have been a very popular lady, she had the nickname of Pops. I was given a number of photographs and reproduce a couple of them in the hope that someone may recognise her.

The girls of Tuxford Hostel, Nottinghamshire. Photograph taken 14 April 1943

WLA Reunion at Southwell Minster - 1996, Ivy 'Pops' Woodliffe, 3rd from left

A steam engine visits Tuxford

Tuxford Hostel, Ivy Woodliffe on right

The Flying Squad - The Tuxford Land Girls

Another undated newspaper cutting, possibly
from the Lincolnshire Echo.

Margaret Fawcett nee McMahon

Margaret McMahon was a waitress at the George Hotel, Halifax, when she decided to join the Land Army.

She was posted to Langtoft near Bourne (Lincs) for the first year, but the fun began once she was posted to Wellingore.

"We were very homesick at first" she said, *"We didn't enjoy it, we didn't know anything, but as we got used it we had a lot of fun even though we had hardly any money"*

Marg was posted to Wellingore Hostel, a building long demolished to make way for new homes. She worked for Eric Parker at Metheringham, Ashby, Digby, Scopwick and Brauncewell.

"The farm workers used to play us up" she said, *"They would hang our bicycles up in the beams and we'd sit down for lunch and find a dead rabbit in our lunch box. We couldn't get back at them, they were too smart for that"*

One of Margaret's first tasks was to learn to ride a bike. *"I was a mass of bruises, I kept falling off in the bushes as I learned to ride up at the Cocked Hat Plantation"* she said.

Entertainment was plentiful. They had an open invitation to dances at RAF Wellingore, and to the camp film shows.

She married the farmer's son, Cyril Fawcett, who died only recently. *"I still keep in touch with some of the* girls", she said.

⋯⋯⋯

For Home and Country.

Arise, oh women of England,
Now that the war is won.
You carried on for the men while they were gone,
But your work has just begun.
Nobly you did your duty
In hospital, factory or field,
You showed your grit and did your bit,
To make the enemy yield.
But it rests with the women of England now,
As they think of the sons they have lost,

To see that their homes and their country
Are worthy of the price they have cost.
Anon.

· · · · · · · ·

Another short article written by Margaret Bell of Branston which appeared in the Spring 2008 issue of 'The Lincolnshire Poacher'

Just a Job For The Girls.

In 1944, myself and two other Women's Land Army girls were employed to work on an arable farm in Lincolnshire.

It was spring time. That March was very dry and the wind was unusually strong. The wind picked up the dry sandy soil from the fields, and it blew in great clouds across the roads, and filled the ditches.

A small stocky man named Jim Mason was employed to dig grips, or narrow trenches, deep down, for him to put in the gripping pipes.

The pipes were stacked, ready for collection, in a pile by the roadside, a mile along the road from the farm.

We girls had to take the great Shire horses and carts to collect the gripping pipes. They were earthenware, heavy, awkward and likely to get broken. We stacked them carefully into the carts, and then made our way along the road, back to the farm in the howling wind.

Through the gate, across the grass field, leading the horses along the ruts, to where Jim was working. Then on his instruction we unloaded the pipes into piles, along where we would be working, in rows across the field.

Using a special narrow spade, he dug a narrow trench, and then, with a different tool with a single tine, he picked up each drainage pipe, and laid it neatly at the end of the previous one.

Slowly he moved across the fields from early morning to teatime, for weeks.

The wind was so strong we could lean against it. Jim Mason advised us to get into the trench and cover our heads with our smocks, but it was no good so we left Jim and led the poor horses home to the farm, took them out of carts and they trotted thankfully into their stables. When their gear was removed, they shook themselves. Their eyes (and ours) were caked with sand and very sore. We offered water, gave them a quick rub down with a wisp of straw, and handful of corn and some hay and left them to the care of the men.   We collected our cycles and rode two miles home in the gritty wind.

Jim Mason had to fill in the trenches before he left that awful day. Some days earlier, we girls had helped to fill in the trenches, but it was back breaking work.

Some years later I noticed wide strips of golden marigolds growing where the trenches had been dug and the pipes laid, the seed must have been unearthed by the gripping; a lasting memorial for weeks of back breaking work.

Note: This shows the diversity of work undertaken by the girls.

········

The following poem was sent to **Hazel Harris** of Worcester and her friend **Marg.** by a soldier friend named Cliff (surname unknown) sometime in 1939-41 when he worked for a short time on a farm in North Herefordshire prior to his 'call-up'.

There's a fine lot of troops in England today,
And everyone thinks that they're grand.
But if anyone wonders "who's best"? I would say
'Tis the lassies that work on the land.
On farms they work hard in all kinds of weather
In sunshine and snow they're as good.
They've got "guts", yes they're sure tough as leather
Are those lassies that get us our food!
We've soldiers and sailors and airmen as well,
In that land that I'm proud to call home,
But the Women's Land Army will lick 'em to hell
Though they'd be the last ones to say.
They're on at their tasks and they'll pull us right through
This war, if we keep up our heads.
But were it not for the great work that they so proudly do,
We would lose cause we'd run short of bread.

The poem appears in Michael Bentinck's book-**"War Time Women"** Although I have not been able to obtain a copy of the book, **'Land Girls at Work'**, I am led to believe that the following poem came from that publication.

Spoon or Spanner.

In old Civvy Street
I could bake quite a treat
In a truly professional manner.
But whilst there's a war
I can't bake anymore
'Cos I've changed my spoon for a spanner

Now my tarts could delight
They were awfully light
And my cakes – well, I dare bet a tanner
If it wasn't for Huns
They could beat anyone'
But I've now changed my spoon for a spanner.

If the war could be won
On just making a bun,
I know I'd come home with a banner.
But instead I'll come back
Looking awfully black
With no spoon in my hand, but a spanner.

D. Marshall
Yorkshire, North Riding.

· · · · · · · ·

Another snippet from the Land Girl's Handbook
Pages 56 and 57
Wages
The Ministry of Agriculture and Fisheries has laid down. As a condition of Employment of a member of the Women's Land Army, that she should be paid a weekly wage of not less than 32s. if she is 18 or over for a working week of up to 48 hours, with a minimum overtime rate of 8d per hour. If she is billeted in a farmhouse, she must receive a minimum wage of 16s. per week

in addition to free board and lodgings. Of course, if the County rates are higher, higher wages are paid to the volunteer. In some counties, for instance, these are as high as 38s.

Before a volunteer goes on a farm she will be told what is the working week and what is the county rate of wages. She will also be told whether Sunday labour and labour on days of public holiday are counted as ordinary overtime or as overtime on a higher rate.

Holidays.

There are no special Women's Land Army regulations about holidays., with or without pay but where a member of the Army has worked for six months at least 20 miles from her home she becomes entitled to a free journey home at the expense of the Women's Land Army (see Chapter VIII). A volunteer's title to the holiday, however, does depend on the terms of her employment and the arrangements that can be made with her employer.

Sickness and Accidents.

Where a volunteer is employed on a weekly basis, the employer is expected to pay her wage in full if she is absent from work owing to sickness, and until she has given her weeks notice and this has expired.

There is no liability of any sort on the Ministry of Agriculture or on the Women's Land Army in respect of sickness of a member or of any accident she may suffer while in employment.

Employed members of the Women's Land Army who fall sick are treated under the National Health Insurance Scheme (see page 29 of the Handbook).

Where an accident occurs to an employed member of the Women's Land Army in the course of her employment, her claim is against her employer under the terms of the Workmen's Compensation Act. Medical treatment will, of course, be obtained under the National Health Insurance Scheme, and the worker will come within the Emergency Hospital Scheme.

The National Health Insurance Scheme was a contributory scheme – money came directly out of wages. If there was an injury then the claim was directly against the farmer!

Today, the Health and Safety at Work Act may have looked more closely at these regulations but in those unenlightened days, 'was all fair in love and War?'

· · · · · · · ·

Useful hints and tips.

Remedy for roughened hands.

Put one ounce of olive oil and one ounce of chopped beeswax into a jar in the oven until melted. Cool and, when easy to handle, roll into a ball. Rub lightly into the hands after washing. A little oat flour will remove the greasiness.

A little French chalk sprinkled into gum boots help them to slip on and off more easily.

LAND GIRL

MANUAL FOR VOLUNTEERS IN THE WOMEN'S LAND ARMY

W.E.SHEWELL-COOPER

ENGLISH UNIVERSITIES PRESS

. . . .

This poem was given to me by an ex. Land girl. Although it cannot be attributed to the Land Army and the author is unknown, I couldn't resist including it as typical of the type of humour a lot of these ladies still possess.

A Hand in the Bird.

I'm a maiden, who is forty,
And a maiden I'll remain.
There are some who call me haughty'
But I care not what they say.

I was running the tombola
At out church bazaar today,
And doing it with gusto
In my usual jolly way....

When suddenly, I know not why,
There came a funny feeling
Of something crawling up my thigh!
I nearly hit the ceiling.

A mouse! I thought, How foul" How mean!
How exquisitely tickly!
Quite soon I know I'm going to scream
I've got to catch it quickly.

I made a grab, I caught the mouse,
Now right inside my knickers
A mouse my foot! It was a HAND!
Great Scot! It was the vicar's!
Anon.

· · · · · · · ·

A final offering from **Marie Bannister** nee DeWael of Branston.
For years I worked upon the land
At a place they call The Mere.
It's a charming little corner,
Where friends are most sincere.
I never will forget those days.
My friends who were so kind
For a boss as good as Patrick Dean
Is very hard to find.
Whenever you're in trouble
He's there to lend a hand.
I thank him for the Happy years
I worked upon his land.
Marie Bannister.

Note. The Mere was Marie's first hostel when she arrived in Lincolnshire and I understand that the above poem still hangs on the farmhouse wall. Marie worked on the land until she was well into her seventies!

· · · · · · · ·

The third and final story from **Margaret Bell** of Branston is about the Lincolnshire village of Mareham and life there during wartime.

Wartime Mareham.

I had been a seamstress in a hot steamy laundry before being catapulted into rural Lincolnshire in 1943 as a Land Girl cycling to work in all weathers, to work in the fields of arable crops and with horses, cows, pigs and hens. I'm sure I must have caused some comments: a white faced skinny girl in jodhpurs, thick socks and heavy shoes, trying to be a farm worker.

We were lodged in Mareham le Fen and treated kindly. The village had two pubs, two grocery shops, two bakeries and two butchers. And, of course, a blacksmith's shop, for shoeing those huge Shire horses which were used to work the light-soiled potato land, a warm place for onlookers. The smell of the scorched hoof stays with me to this day.

The village hall, built after the previous war, was a meeting place for clubs, for dances and for family celebrations and occasionally for films. The lovely sand stone church of St. Helen on the north side of the village catered for a congregation from far and near. The vicar and his wife worked hard to help on every occasion, including sick visiting and some school lessons. The children had days off in the autumn to help with the potato harvest.

Many of the villagers were farm worker who walked or cycled to work. Most of the farms were arable and grew potatoes, sugar beet and corn. Winter was the time to clear the ditches, trim hedges and lead root crops to feed the animals. Many of the wives worked seasonally, 9am to 3.30pm setting potatoes.

Singling tiny seedlings of sugar beet, row after seemingly endless row was a back breaking job and later picking the lovely new potatoes into big baskets. When the children were small they went with their parents and played in the fields, with lunch packed in a tin, along with a flask or a bottle of cold tea.

When I first met those women they wore long dresses and cotton bonnets, but later they copied the Land Girls and wore overalls and head scarves. Gloves were scorned unless working stony land. Always cheery, they were fond of the latest gossip.

Rabbits made a useful addition to the menu and the skins were sold to the tinkers who called occasionally. Many families kept a pig in a sty at the end of the garden and fed it on scraps, plus meal allowed by the pig club. A lovely little pink pig could squeal very loudly, and as well as feeding them someone had to clear out the pig muck and carry in the straw bedding. How well I remember chasing four little piglets that had jumped the sty fence and escaped. We ran after them across roads, dykes, fields and hedges. We laughed later but it wasn't funny at the time.

When it was time to 'put down' the fattened pig, the wives co-operated to make sausages and pies. The hams and fitches were salted in huge troughs; lard was rendered from the lumps of fat and poured into large white pails for future use.

Monday was wash day. The copper in the outhouse was filled with rainwater and the fire lit. The clothes were boiled, rinsed and blued and the table-cloths starched. Then they were pegged on the clothesline to blow in the wind. They smelt lovely when brought into the house, especially in winter. One could almost smell the Arctic.

On Saturday the home-made slip mats were taken out to be shaken and the floor washed, and the furniture polished with home-made beeswax. Baking was done before the weekend ready for Sunday's special tea – trays of jam tarts, scones and slab cakes. The kitchens smelt lovely and were warm when the fire was stoked up to heat the side oven. Many meals were cooked on the fire in huge saucepans with one or two steamers above. – boiled bacon and two vegetables, rabbit and stew, the top steamer apple or jam suet pudding.

Every cottage had a vegetable garden, for potatoes, carrots and greens and always a row of kidney beans. Flowers were propagated by exchanging cuttings, with roses a great favourite.

In May, the nearby woods had a carpet of lily of the valley, gathered in bunches, enclosed in a sheaf of leaves. The perfume was overpowering. I remember cycling with several bunches hanging from the handlebars for distribution to friends and neighbours. Also growing wild were narcissi with the pheasant eye, also exquisitely perfumed. And the tall hedges were covered with wild roses and honeysuckle.

Where the lilies grew were the woods of slim silver birch, which were trimmed every few years and the tops bundled up for kindling. In other woods the oak and the ash were felled and led out by teams of heavy horses. The busy wood-yard in the village echoed to the whining of saw benches, with saw dust piled high. In the carpenter's shop, men worked with saw, plane and chisel, making ladders, farm equipment and thatching pegs.

Our pleasure time was to walk out in our Sunday best, especially if the sun shone, or go to the nearest town to shop, or visit a market or an auction. Occasionally we went to the pictures or a dance at the village hall. The men played bowls on the green near the hall, or darts at the pub, and supported the local football team.

The Silver Prize Band was what the people loved most. Formed after the First World War by men who came back from the trenches, the band played at all the village fetes and celebrations. It gained itself a considerable reputation.

Italian and German prisoners of war from the camp at Moorsby travelled to work on farms in open back lorries. We could hear them coming, singing opera songs. They liked having fun, stole eggs and in the camp they made rings from old saucepans and sandals from old rope. The German PoWs worked the best but were more solemn.

The Land Girls had been taken into village homes and several stayed and married local men. When the war ended I stayed to live among my village friends. We watched the changes from horses to tractor, binders to combine harvesters and in the home to the labour saving devices we now take for granted.

St Helen's Church

Beetroot for Breakfast!

I saw the following poem in a book entitled 'Digging for Memories'-
The Women's Land Army on Cornwall, (edited by Melissa Hardy) and I
thought it could apply to almost all retired land girls everywhere.

Cool Grandma.

What did you do in the war, Grandma?
We're learning about it at school.
Were you a WAAF or an ATS or a Wren?
They looked so cool.

Haven't they taught you about the land?
How the men had to go and fight,
How thousands of girls, from cities and towns,
Became farmers overnight.

We were the Women's Land Army,
Eighty thousand strong.
We worked all hours in the heat and the cold,
Each day was hard and long.

We dug the ditches, milked the cows
Brought in the harvest grain.
Collected the eggs and killed the rats!
We braved the wind and rain.

A Cinderella Army,
We weren't asked to the Ball.
But aching backs and weary limbs
Were remembered by us all.

Yet through the hardship and the toil
We did our very best.
A job well done was our reward
And never mind the rest.
That's what we did in the war, child,
So tell your friends at school
They won't see us in the Big Parade,
But Land Girls, we were cool"
Hilda Gibson. 1999 - Cornwall.

This poem was written by Jean Taylor of Arnold who submitted a newspaper cutting of a short story about her mother **Mavis Maltby** who had served in the Land Army. Unfortunately I have no information about her service with the Land Army.

Fifty years ago, the war came to an end
There were street parties, joy, laughter and tears
Everyone was everyone's friend
Remembering what they'd been through.
Years thirty-nine to forty five
They had spirit, guts and strength
It was hard to just survive.
The loss of life, the bombings, folk had to move away.
The ration books, the starving, would they see another day?
There'll always be an England. It kept them smiling through.
Dig for Victory. Waste Not, Want Not
Mend it, patch it, it'll do.
Rabbit pie, lentil soup and braised liver
Menus you might just see
But rations were very limited
One egg a month for tea!
Evacuation for little children
To the country out of the way,
Some went abroad to be safer
While others in Nottingham did stay.
Blackouts and air raid precautions, everyone had to muck in,
Collecting saucepans to make spitfires, winning the war was everything.
To fly the Union Jack, red, white and blue to see.
We are proud of those who fought for us, to bring us victory.
Everyone who played a part in war has a story to tell
Of how they were poor, how they struggled to keep us free
They did their best for you and me.
My dear Mum and Dad helped in the war,
They've passed away now, but had stories to tell
Of death and destruction, a living hell.
Life's easy now you have to agree
Life was lost to save you and me.
Jean Taylor.

Beetroot for Breakfast!

To commemorate the disbandment of the Women's Land Army a special **SUPPER PARTY** was held at the Albert Hall Institute, Nottingham on 7th October 1950. The Chairman on this occasion was Lady Sibell Argyles and Long Service Armlets were presented by Miss Amy Curtis,C.B.E, (Chief Administrative Officer , Women's Land Army.)

It is interesting to see the menu for this occasion ;
Soup, Boiled York Ham, Salad, French Pastries, Fresh Pineapple and Cream, Tea or coffee. The evening concluded with community singing and Auld Lang Syne. In July 1954 food rationing was finally lifted.

A Supper Party held at the Albert Hall Institute, Nottingham October 1950. One Land girl who attended was Margaret Parrot nee Oldham (4th from left)

Celebration.

On 3.30pm on Saturday 17th June 1995 a Service of Thanksgiving was held at Southwell Minster, Nottinghamshire
This Women's Land Army Celebration Service was held just 50 years after the end of the Second World War.

During the service a brief outline of the History of the Women's Land Army was given by Mrs Jean Proctor of the British Women's Land Army Society. The Choir was drawn from the churches throughout Nottinghamshire and belonged to the Royal School of Church Music. The Welcome and Opening Prayer was taken by The Provost, The Very Rev'd David Leaning.

The following day on Sunday 18th June a ceremonial tree planting took place at Rufford Country Park when an English Oak was planted by Mrs Jean Proctor. (I visited the Oak tree in February this year (2010) and unfortunately the commemorative place has disappeared)
This was followed by a fly past of the Battle of Britain Memorial Wing.

There was also a nostalgic display of War-time Farming Equipment at Rufford Mill Exhibition Centre on the theme of the Fire Service during the war years.

Nearing the end.

The Women's Land Army was terminated in October 1950 and the following speech was made by **Her Majesty the Queen** on the occasion of the Farewell Parade on Saturday October 21st 1950. Buckingham Palace.

"I am very pleased to have this opportunity of speaking to the Women's Land Army, whose Patron I have been for the past nine years.

A Farewell Parade always has something about it that is sad, but when it marks the culmination of a long and honourable history, our feelings are chiefly of pride and gratitude. This is certainly so today.

The story of the Land Army has been one of great response by the women of our country in the nation's hour of danger and need.

They could not have done more for their country than they did. By their efforts they helped to ensure that our country contributed its utmost towards its food supplies and for this the nation owes them an everlasting debt.

The Women's Army has always been recruited from volunteers, and I like to think that its greatest strength lay in the free spirit which has always inspired the people of these Islands to their greatest achievements.

The Land Army attracted girls from every kind of different occupation and I have always admired their courage in responding so readily to a call which they knew must bring them not only hardship and sometimes loneliness, but often danger.

By their hard work and patient endurance they earned a noble share in the immense effort which carried our country to victory. Yet their real task did not end when the war was over, for they stayed at their posts through the difficult years that followed.

Five thousand of those who served in the Land Army have decided to remain on the land. There can be no greater tribute than this to the happiness with which their work rewarded them.

Now the time has come to say good-bye, because the job has been done, but the sadness which many will feel at the parting, should be outweighed by pride in the achievement. Moreover, the Land Army will not, in any case, be only an affectionate memory, since it will live in the shape of thousands of members who have settled down in the countryside as the wives of farmers and farm workers, or who are themselves continuing to work in agriculture when the Organisation itself comes to an end.

I thank you all for the splendid service you have given your country. In field and forest, garden and orchard and dairy, the work of the Women's Land Army has always been worthy of the ageless traditions of those who have toiled for the land they loved. I know the whole nation will join me in wishing you all good fortune for the future"

After speaking with a friend I learned that his mother had been in the Land Army and served in Nottinghamshire. Unfortunately his mother passed away and very little of her time in the Land Army has been remembered or recorded. However, she became pregnant to an American GI who was locally stationed and John Woolley has recorded his efforts to trace his father over the years. Similar circumstances may have occurred to other land girls but I wonder how many did manage to trace their fathers. Here then is a resume of John's letter regarding his mother.

Doris (Val) Woolley.   **Daybrook, Nottingham**
"Further to our conversation regarding my mother and her wartime employment in the Land Army, much of what she said is very sketchy. However, over the years just a few fragments of information came out

regarding the days she worked on the land helping to supply the needs of the nation during those food scarcity years. I believe the lack of my mother reliving her memories of those wartime years were due to some being unpleasant ones. I trust therefore that what little information I can supply may be of use.

Mum mentioned she worked at a farm in Bunny (Nottinghamshire) and she cycled there, however, I'm not too certain if that was to arrive on a Monday and sleep over at the Bunny farm until her weekly shift had ended. She also mentioned that whilst harvesting a root vegetable (one presumes Beet) she nearly took her fingers off whilst chopping the soiled root and leaf part of the vegetable, she mentioned she had to have immediate medical attention to stop the bleeding. Mother continued to work after this accident but kept the scars as proof the rest of her life.

I can recall her saying that farm work was very hard and she and others were out in all types of weather and were not treated well by some land owners, her thoughts at the time regarding this was, that some farmers thought that only men and boys should work on the land.

I don't know the length of Mum's wartime Land Army employment but it came to a halt in 1944 after she became pregnant to an American GI stationed locally at the Apollo Table Water Factory which was part of the Home Brewery complex in Daybrook. Her father was working there at that time as a drayman and continued there until his retirement in the 1960s.

Mum was always displeased that any governing government since the World War II had not recognised the need to honour Land Army girls with a medal. Unfortunately, Mum died just short of this recognition and we received no medal.

To add to this, is the story of me eventually finding my American kin. This story could be included if you should find it of interest but it all stemmed from my mother's time in the Land Army.

For most of my early childhood I was brought up by my grandparents. The only time I was aware of my American parentage was when I left school in 1959 when, at that time, one had to show their birth certificate to the Headmaster as proof of age The Headmaster Mr Weddle of Redhill School, Arnold, declined my birth certificate as the surname on it was different to the name I had used throughout my school life. Being born a war baby I had taken my family surname and I was unaware that my mother had married in 1947 and that the person she had married was not my natural father, I was given his surname, but was not adopted.

The need to contact my American father never materialised until the middle 1970s having settled down in marriage and finding time to assess the situation of who and where my American father was. Having been told my father's full name and his approximate date of birth and the part of the States that my mother thought he lived, my quest began"

John then gave a full account of his contacts and enquiries with numerous organisations both in this country and in the United States, in his quest to find his father. Some were very helpful whilst other were less so. After prolonged enquiries and many 'no trace' replies from several sources John got the break-through he needed and his quest became a roller coaster of good news and in November 2001, almost a quarter of a century after taking the first steps to trace his father, he set foot on American soil.

John continues his story, *"21ˢᵗ November 2001 was for me memorable because it was the day I finally met my American kin for the first time. I shall never forget my first sighting of my Aunt Donna and her husband Sam as we drove onto their driveway, seeing them standing together holding hands and awaiting our arrival. I was last out of the car and finally embraced my Aunt and I apologised for my long absence as tear of joy ran down both our faces followed by smiles that continued through-out the long warm afternoon.*

Those moments I shall treasure for life and it just goes to prove that if one follows their dreams, they can come true."

Since that first visit in 2001, John and his wife have travelled to see their American kin every year, and says John *"whilst I have breath and the finances , I shall continue to journey across the pond to embrace the family I never knew I had prior to leaving school in 1959"*

Note. As a footnote to his story John wrote the following, *"Unbeknown to me just two years before my quest started my father had died in 1972 of a heart attack at the age of 49. Alas also, my three younger American brothers all died tragically before I set foot on American soil. Had the American government given me information on first enquiry regarding the wartime address of my father in Mendenhall MS, I would have been able to embrace my three brothers, but it was not to be."*

Talking with John and listening to his story, coupled with the letter he wrote to me made me wonder just how many other people's lives may have been affected by wartime relationships in similar circumstances. I know there were many happy results from many liaisons as letters and interviews in previous pages of this book have proved. It is a great shame that no more information of his mother Doris Woolley and her service in the Land Army is known but I think John proved his commitment in tracing his family over the 25 year period.

The Women's Timber Corps. (The Lumberjills)

The WTC (Women's Timber Corps) was a section of the Women's Land Army and like the Land Army received no official recognition for its work during the war. Similarly the WTC was not represented on Armistice Day at the Cenotaph and had no separate wreath.

Today, in the Queen Elizabeth Forest Park near Aberfoyle in Scotland stands a life-size bronze statue of a member of the WTC, a lasting memorial to those girls who toiled in the forests, sometimes in remote areas to provide much needed timber for the war effort.

The memorial was created by Fife based artist, Malcolm Robertson and was unveiled by Environment Minister Michael Russell on 10 October 2007.

(Facts from the Dunoon and Argyleshire Standard 10 October 2007)

The Memorial to the Women's Timber Corps situated in the Queen Elizabeth Forest Park near Aberfoyle, Sterlingshire, Scotland

Whilst researching the above I came across two poems which reflect the work and feelings of members of the WTC which I think will appeal to anyone who served with the WTC.

Forester's
They're tramping through the forest
They're brushing past the undergrowth
They have but one desire
They're greatest thought, their highest aim,
To see in Britain, Peace again
They have no tanks or rifles,
They have no stripes or drill,
They have no ships or aeroplanes

205

But Britain needs them still,
They're fighting hard with axe and saw
They're Britain's Women's Timber Corps'.
They're proud of their profession,
Bad weather does not count;
They bring the tall trees crashing down
The piles of pit props mount,
They're doing their bit to win the war
This almost unknown 'Timber Corps'
By J I Melvin

· · · · · · · ·

The Other Way

There is a land, or so I'm told,
Where timber girls ne'er feel the cold,
Where trees come down all shed and peeled,
And there's no need an axe to wield.
The transport's never broken down,
And Jill goes every night to town.
How different here in snow and sleet,
Shivering with wet and frozen feet.
But wait. The sun's come out at last,
The summer's here and winter's past,
The lumberjills work all the day –
Who'd have it round that other way?
By Hilton Wood

· · · · · · · ·

Many of the ex. Land girls to whom I have spoken have told me of the enjoyment and excitement they experienced when they attended the special reunion occasions and celebrations which were held in Lincolnshire and Nottinghamshire. I am grateful to **Margaret Bell of Branston** for sending me an order of service for 'A Service of Celebration of the work of the Women's Land Army' which was held in Lincoln Cathedral on Sunday 25th January 2009 at 11.15am. I think it only fitting to finish with a resume of that service.

Introduction.

In December, 2007 the Department for Food and Rural Affairs (DEFRA) announced the award of a specially designed badge and certificate for surviving members of the Women's Land Army and the Women's Timber Corps in recognition and commemoration of their efforts during the Second World War and its aftermath. The application process was launched at the end of January, 2008 and there was a huge interest in the badge... DEFRA has now despatched badges and certificates to over 30,000 ladies. A national award ceremony took place at 10 Downing Street, London on 23 July, 2008 when fifty ladies, selected at random from those that had applied, were presented with their badge by Hilary Benn, Secretary of State, and they all had the opportunity to meet the Prime Minister.

Given the limited number of ladies who were able to attend the 10 Downing Street event, Ministers were keen that a series of regional events should take place during the autumn/ winter 2008 in order to honour more of the large number of veterans that had applied for the badge. Within Lincolnshire, North Lincolnshire and North-East Lincolnshire over 700 ladies were eligible for the award. Her Majesty The Queen indicated that her Lords-Lieutenant should be involved in organising these events and that each event would provide an opportunity to celebrate the award of the badge and to commemorate the efforts of the members of the Women's Land Army and Timber Corps.

It is therefore, with the kind support of the Dean and Chapter of Lincoln, that Her Majesty's Lord Lieutenant of Lincolnshire, Mr Tony Worth, invites you all today to acknowledge and celebrate the role played by the ladies of the Women's Land Army and the Women's Timber Corps during World War II and its aftermath.

· · · · · · · ·

Hymn – 'All people that on earth do dwell'.

Welcome – The Bidding by Rev. Canon Gavin Kirk, Precentor of Lincoln and Canon-in-Residence, welcomes the congregation and leads the Bidding.

The contribution of the Armed Forces and other uniformed organisations to World War II has been clearly recognised. But many others gave up their home lives, their freedom and their security to serve on (what we call) the Home Front. They included the Women's Land Army and Timber Corps, the miners and Bevan Boys who worked underground, the munitions and industrial workers, whose factories were often the targets for enemy bombers, and many other civilians. Some were volunteers others were conscripted. Their courage and quiet dedication kept this country going through the darkest days of the war.

Those people and organisations were not formally recognised and thanked by the nation at that time, and we owe it to them to do so now. We are indeed grateful to them; many of them were then young; most are now entering old age. They set aside their personal ambitions and plans for the common good, and thereby set an example for our society. We now look to the younger generation to take up that tradition of service to the common good.

St Paul wrote, "Let each of you look not to your own interests, but to the interests of others." In gratitude to our heavenly Father for the past and in trust for the future, let us commit ourselves to the service of God and neighbour.

All. – Almighty God, we thank you for all those who, without earthly recognition, gave themselves for the common good during the Second World War. Help us, like them, to look to the interests of others before our own, following the example of Jesus, your Son, who suffered and died for us, yet lives and reigns with you and the Holy Spirit, one God, now and forever.

Hymn – 'God is working his purpose out as year succeeds year.'
Dedication of Badges – The Lord Lieutenant speaks to veterans of the W.L.A. on behalf of H.M The Queen.
Hymn – 'I vow to thee my country.'
Close – The National Anthem.

Similar services were held in many counties throughout the country.

LINCOLN CATHEDRAL

A Service of Celebration
of the work of the
WOMEN'S LAND ARMY

Sunday, 25th January, 2009
11.15 am
The Conversion of St Paul

The Final Word

There are hundreds of stories still to be told of the lives of the girls who helped to save Britain in the hard years of World War II. Many of those stories will go unrecorded and that is a great shame as they have so much to tell.

I would like to apologise to those who I have been unable to visit for one reason or another and I feel that time is catching up with all of us now. I hope that they will tell their families of their experiences and leave a wealth of history for others to enjoy. The Women's Land Army is fast becoming a forgotten organisation and any oral reminisces should be converted to written records before it's too late. To have served in the Land Army was a unique experience and as such the knowledge of those six years of working on the land during WWII should be left for future generations to read and understand and to hope that they will never have to experience the causes ever again.

Once again I would like to say **'Thank you'** to all the ladies who gave their time and took the trouble to talk to me. I was always made welcome and I have enjoyed meeting everyone. I have made a lot of friends and my wife and I still enjoy seeing some of these ladies from time to time.

The Women's Land Army was excluded from marching in the Remembrance Day Parade at the Cenotaph until the year 2000, when it was included – to march at the back.

When the ended in 1945 and on disbandment of the Land Army, the girls returned their uniform clothing and received no civvies, no gratuities and no medals. Recruitment posters showed <u>FOUR</u> women's services, the WAAFS, ATS, WRENS, and the WLA all marching together, shoulder to shoulder under the flag.

The Women of World War II Memorial in Whitehall, London

Beetroot for Breakfast!

On the 9th July 2005, Her Majesty Queen Elizabeth II unveiled a memorial to **THE WOMEN OF WORLD WAR II** which stands in Whitehall, London about 100 yards from the Cenotaph.

The four faces of the Women's War Memorial in Whitehall.

The Four Faces of the Women's War Memorial in Whitehall continued

Bibliography and Further Reading

Women in the First World War. Gill Thomas.
Cambridge University Press. 1989.

Land Army Days. **Cinderellas of the Soil**. Knighton Joyce. Aurora
Publishing. 1994.

They Fought in the Fields. Nicola Tyrer. Sinclair Stevenson. 1996.

The Land Army - A portrait. Gill Clarke. Sansom & Company. 2008.

War Time Women. Michael Bentinck. Pub. Michael Bentinck. 1998.

Nottinghamshire Air Crashes. David Needham.
Landmark Publishing. 2008.

Digging for Memories. Melissa Hardie. The Hypatia Trust, Penzance,
Cornwall. 2006.

Addendum

As time passes, all our memories grow dim and time and places sometimes become confused or even lost. With added pleasures like the conditions of war time it isn't always easy to make clear definition regarding certain facts. Most of the memories included in this book have been authenticated as far as possible but one experience has to be clarified.

The twin stones of the Memorial commemorating the two Lancaster bombers that crashed in January 1945. The memorial is situated on the Trent Valley Way, besides the River Trent, at Hoveringham, Nottinghamshire.

After closing the pages of research on this book, certain facts have been revealed. I refer to the account of the two crashed Lancaster bombers given by Mrs Joyce Truman of Lowdham on page 83. I have commented on the facts that no lives were lost in the two bomber crashes at Syerston Airfield in 1943, as confirmed in David Needham's book, 'Nottinghamshire Air Crashes' (2008). I am now able to give details of two further Lancaster bombers which crashed in January 1945 and are the two to which Joyce Truman refers.

New information, only recently revealed is the result of research by Lady Helen Nall and her husband Sir Edward Nall who own land situated at Hoveringham, Nottinghamshire, near the River Trent and the site of the two crashes which occurred only 17 days apart. Lady Nall was using a metal detector on the land when she discovered some aircraft debris which was later confirmed as from the two latter crashes mentioned. In both cases the aircraft exploded and the entire crews of each aircraft were lost – a total of 14 crew members.

On Sunday 30th May 2010, a memorial ceremony dedicated to the crews was held near the crash site and was attended by families and relatives of the crews from Canada, New Zealand, Australia and the UK. 13 of the 14 families involved attended the ceremony and it is with thanks to the tireless research and work of Lady Nall that made this possible.

If you would like to read more about these incidents then Lady Helen Nall has produced a book entitled 'The Courage of the Small Hours' with all the profits going to the RAF Benevolent Fund and the Bomber Command Memorial Appeal.